THE
NO-FUSS
FAMILY
COOKBOOK

THE NO-FUSS FAMILY COOKBOOK

simple recipes for everyday life

RYAN SCOTT

PHOTOGRAPHY BY CHRIS ANDRE

Houghton Mifflin Harcourt

Boston   New York   2021

For information about permissions to reproduce selections from
this book, write to trade.permissions@hmhco.com or to Permissions,
Houghton Mifflin Harcourt Publishing Company, 3 Park Avenue,
19th Floor, New York, New York 10016.

hmhbooks.com

Library of Congress Cataloging-in-Publication Data is available.
ISBN 978-0-358-43914-1 (hbk)
ISBN 978-0-358-43912-7 (ebk)

Book design by Ashley Lima

Printed in the USA
1 2021
4500823049

To Olive, our "baby burrito," the best decision of our lives. I wrote this book for you as a sort of "culinary family history" in the hopes that you would share these recipes and stories with your future family. For the Scotts, food is and always has been a catalyst for amazing times, memories, conversations, and love. I'll look forward to you adding your own chapters someday.

XOXO,
Daddy

contents

foreword

Hootie Hoo, friends!

Ryan and I are both members of a lifelong club: the Top Chef "fraternity." He was a contestant the season before I was cast, and I remember watching him on the show and being captivated by his charisma (and his "fancy" poached pears). Now that I know him well, I know that Ryan is anything but fancy—he's a no-fuss, no-frills kind of guy. It's hard to understand the connectedness of those of us in the Top Chef "world" unless you have experienced it. I can walk up to anyone who has ever been on Top Chef, no matter how long they were on the show, and whether or not I know them personally, and we'd feel an instant connection. There would be mutual admiration for what we went through in the amazing (and grueling) experience. I'm so glad that Top Chef brought Ryan and me together.

I first met Ryan when we were attending an awards show back in 2008. His big smile and warmth struck me right away. Seeing a big, muscle-y man who was truly comfortable exuding a warm, "female" energy—the kind that draws you in and makes you feel at home—was so cool. Ryan is the perfect blend of all of my favorite energies, and for a guy like him to be front and center in his industry while showing vulnerability and sensitivity as a father—it's huge and empowering for men and women alike.

When Ryan and I did a culinary event together in Yosemite along with chef Ariane Duarte, I had my first chance to work with him directly. We had a blast. We really forged our friendship over that long weekend, and Ryan and my husband, Matthew, hit it off instantly as well. There's nothing better than seeing your partner enjoying your friend as much as you do. I knew I had found someone pretty darn special. I mean, Matthew attended Ryan and Lesley's destination wedding, alone (I was doing a shoot), so it was clear that Matthew's people-radar was spot-on-accurate and agreed with mine: Ryan was a keeper!

Through the years of our friendship I have seen Ryan traverse the world of dating, find "the one," marry the love of his life, and then dive head-first into life as a family man who is completely gaga over being a dad. In this book, Ryan makes a bold statement to parents and especially to dads—one that will resonate with so many, whether you are a new dad, a seasoned father, or a single dad raising kids on your own. The *No-Fuss Family*

Cookbook's photography, narrative, and vibe convey an easygoing message that will not force anyone into any sort of box. His universal approach to cooking is to do it with intention, love, and a big dose of fun . . . all while making it "no-fuss," because as we know, life can get pretty crazy!

The timing of this book is especially exciting given that more people are cooking at home and are becoming less intimidated to do so. Ryan has a refreshing way of making people comfortable about "playing" with food and flavors. For those who have just recently found a love for cooking, it says that they too are a part of the "club"—it's not exclusive . . . it's inclusive!   Cooking is, above all, a love-language and a creative process that gives us a way to take back power in our environments. In this book, Ryan gives endless tips and tools that allow us free range when it comes to cooking. He makes it clear that we can do it all AND get food on the table! It's timely and refreshing. Whenever a chef gives you alternatives and ways to personalize a recipe—like in his Banana, Brown Butter Granola, and Yogurt Mash-Up—the practicality and approachability of the recipe will soar. I can't tell you how many times I have bought too many bananas and have been bored to tears with the traditional solutions! As a busy parent, it is all about thinking on your feet and adapting. Ryan does this beautifully and creates pure magic.

As someone who loves to bake (and in an industry where many women gravitate towards the pastry side of things), I love that Ryan gives us a generous serving of his love for baking within these pages.

I love seeing my stepson and nephew starting to explore the world of cooking. As soon as I read this book, I knew that it would be a fabulous tool for both of them. It's not intimidating or filled with rigid, unfamiliar terms or instructions.

It's also not your typical, male-authored cookbook with the stereotypical color palette of masculinity. This book is bright, colorful (Ryan loves pink!), imaginative, casual, and playful. It invites you to explore its pages and will make you smile. We should be happy when we cook, and happy in the kitchen. After all, it's a love language! This book belongs in a happy kitchen.

I absolutely love this book. It is approachable, fun, joy-inspiring, and practical. It highlights and fulfills the need for easy solutions and for connecting with your loved ones through food. It takes the craziness of family life and family meals and makes them no-fuss. This book is, in my opinion, perfect.

Hugs and Spices,
Carla Hall

introduction

From recipes for protein-loving omnivores to ones for my very Zen vegans and test-of-time vegetarians, this cookbook dips its toe into every culinary pool. In other words, this is not a "single note" cookbook. Whether you need a quick solution to feed last-minute guests or a snack to offer to the preschoolers invading your home for a playdate, I have you covered. In this collection, you'll find relatable tips and hacks to help you minimize your culinary path of destruction (aka massive cleanup), as well as recipes that freeze well for later. But what really makes this book different from my last is an evolution that has happened over the past several years—one that led me into a new role as "Dad." When I am asked, "Who is Ryan Scott?" my answer has many parts. I am Olive's father, and husband to my awesome wife, Lesley. I'm a "doggy daddy" to Teddy and Pumpkin (call that cheesy or whatever you want, but my pups kinda own me). I'm a chef/baker, business owner, and restaurateur. I'm a cookbook author (*One to Five*), TV personality (are you guys tired of me yet?), family member, friend, and go-to kind of guy. But in all honesty, it is because of those first two titles—"Daddy" and "hubby"—that this book came to be and has now ended up on your kitchen counter.

Within these pages, I incorporate ways you can get your kids involved in the cooking process by offering opportunities for them to give mixtures a stir or to assemble easy dishes alongside you. I love assigning Olive little tasks that make cooking fun and set her up for success, whether it is by having her wash (unbreakable) dishes or asking her to help "set the table" by putting out our napkins. I'll teach you my "sheet pan method," which turns out the most amazing roasted vegetables you have ever tasted, and walk you through ways to customize a recipe to your family's taste. I provide nonstandard substitution suggestions that can broaden the appeal of a dish or help you reflect the current season with your choice of produce. You'll find a number of recipes that are portable and single-portion-size that can really save you in a pinch as a snack, meal on the go, or backup reassurance in the freezer. These important components can lessen the stress and craziness of what-the-heck-am-I-going-to-make-for-dinner weekday evenings. No matter *what* amount of time you have in the hustle of your daily life, the practice of cooking for tomorrow *today* is a kind of insurance policy that is worth your investment. I'll walk you through how to make your recipes serve #DoubleDuty for more than one meal. With anecdotes and narratives from my life of growing up in

California, my time in culinary school, and the years I have been with my wife, I'll take you on a food-driven journey, and eventually, we'll arrive at the current state of things: my life as a dad, family man, and full-time working/traveling parent. Even if you cannot find the time to travel, the recipes in this book offer you a culinary passport to the destination of your choosing, geographically or in state of mind.

As a chef, my passion lies in having everyday home cooks whip up my recipes. As a dad and husband, having delicious, easy, and broadly appealing recipes at my fingertips is essential. I enjoy making a mix of healthy recipes (like my "Perfect" Asparagus with Pistachio Pistou, page 185) and ones that are a bit more indulgent (like my "Cheat Day" Spatchcock Chili Dogs with Super-Easy Cheese Sauce, page 153, or my Foolproof Gooey Brownies, page 232), depending on my family's mood. I have you covered in both the cravings and the "healthy meal for the family" departments! Sharing recipes with other busy fams is my *jam* (strawberry, grape, pick your favorite). I cook for my family any time I'm not traveling for work or working late.

My daughter has been by my side in the kitchen since she was super-small (and in a baby seat). I have loved being able to introduce her to new culinary aromas. My friend Lidia Bastianich gave me a great tip soon after Olive was born. She suggested that I take an ingredient (such as basil) from whatever recipe I was cooking, warm it up in my hands, and put it under Olive's nose so that she could be introduced to the ingredient long before she ever tasted it. This created familiarity with ingredients and a positive first experience of these foods for Olive. It has allowed us to add a wider variety of ingredients to dishes *sooner* and, so far, has resulted in a not-very-picky kiddo!

Olive now loves to "help" me any time she can, and although having a toddler as a sous chef sometimes makes cooking look like a comedy routine, I love being able to share my passion with her. Cooking with her and sharing these moments has created invaluable opportunities for daddy-daughter bonding. It has broadened my perspective on family meals, while simultaneously simplifying *and* helping me narrow down my ultimate goal: getting food on the table. It is all about creating *one* dish or meal that works for *every* person in the family (plus, less work for the person who is left doing the dishes!). I'm pretty sure that being a short-order cook at home isn't anyone's cup of tea!

At the risk of sounding like a dorky dad quoting a Disney movie, "Anyone can cook!" (Thanks, *Ratatouille*—it's been on repeat at our house for a week.) It really is the truth! Whether I'm doing a live cooking demo or a culinary TV segment, my goal is always the same: to get people to realize that they *can* cook and get a meal on the table! No matter their time constraints or level of expertise, there will always be a recipe that can serve them well. That's where *The No-Fuss Family Cookbook* comes in. Here is a collection of go-to recipes that have come straight from my home kitchen, where they're in regular rotation—from years of trial and error, influences from my travels, adaptations of favorite recipes from my childhood, and the mother of all invention: necessity! These versatile recipes are made from easily accessible ingredients and feature a wide range of prep and cooking times. I'm here to (gently) push you out of your culinary comfort zone and introduce you to some members of your new go-to ingredient gang, including miso, quinoa, coconut oil, and all types of vinegars. If some of these sound a bit unfamiliar, I'll teach you how to use them well and make them appeal to kids and adults alike (Olive crosses her heart).

Family life, though wonderful, can be a very messy business—but worrying about what meals to make does not have to be a contributor to the madness. So wipe your mind clear of the intimidating cookbooks or recipes you have avoided in the past, and sink right into the no-fuss way of family cooking.

breakfast and baked goods

olive's naturally sweet pb&j pancakes

Prep Time: 5 minutes | Cook Time: 20 to 30 minutes

MAKES 12 PANCAKES

½ cup whole wheat flour

1 teaspoon baking powder

1 teaspoon baking soda

½ teaspoon salt

2 overripe medium bananas (about ¾ cup mashed)

½ cup smooth peanut butter

2 large eggs, at room temperature, lightly beaten

¼ cup whole milk, at room temperature

1 cup fresh blueberries, rinsed and dried

Cooking spray

When I became a dad, I realized how much control parents actually have over what they feed their children, especially in those first years, when kids spend most of their time at home with you. My wife and I are happy to be able to say that aside from Olive's birthday cakes (which are nothing short of sugar gluttony), she doesn't consume much sugar. I'm not saying this to pass judgment on other parents—cross my heart. And really, there are no unrealistic expectations here. You can keep processed sugar out of your little one's diet by using easy-to-come-by and inexpensive ingredients. Don't get me wrong—I have a culinary degree in pastry, and I love sweet flavor profiles, but there are ways to do "sweet" that will also be approved by my daughter's dentist (wink wink). A perfect example of this is my daughter's favorite recipe: PB&J pancakes. The sweetness comes from natural peanut butter and ripe bananas. It's that simple.

In a medium bowl using a whisk, mix the flour, baking powder, baking soda, and salt until thoroughly combined. Set aside.

In a large bowl, mash the bananas until creamy with a few small chunks remaining. Add the peanut butter, eggs, and milk and mix well to combine. Add the flour mixture and stir until just combined; stop mixing when the batter just comes together to avoid overmixing. Gently fold in the blueberries.

Heat a large nonstick skillet over medium heat. Spray the pan with cooking spray. Using a paper towel, carefully wipe the skillet so there is just a bare residue of spray coating the pan. Reduce the heat to medium-low.

continued

olive's naturally sweet pb&j pancakes, continued

Using a 2-ounce scoop or ¼-cup measure, scoop 3 portions of the batter into the skillet, leaving room for them to spread. Cook, undisturbed, until deep brown on the bottom, 5 to 6 minutes, then flip and cook, undisturbed, until cooked through, 5 to 6 minutes more. Repeat with the remaining batter. Serve straight from the skillet or at room temperature.

Notes

⭐ For an on-the-go breakfast, let the pancakes cool on a wire rack, transfer them to a zip-top bag, and freeze. When ready to serve, warm the pancakes in the microwave for 30 seconds, then off you go!

⭐ Don't rush it—low and slow is the way to go to achieve perfect pancakes. Cooking them at too high a temperature will result in underdone pancakes with burnt edges.

ryan's all-in-one savory breakfast bake

Prep Time: 20 minutes | Cook Time: 50 to 60 minutes

As a parent, I try to sneak veggies into as many dishes as possible to give my daughter an extra boost of nutrition. I mean, why not? We are darn lucky that Olive will pretty much eat vegetables in any shape or form, but for those kiddos who won't, give this recipe a shot. The sweet corn in the custard camouflages the taste of any other veggies in the recipe.

We pretty much *always* have company at our house, and often overnight. And although I am a chef, I refuse to be a short-order cook in my own kitchen, so this one-pan dish is the perfect solution for pleasing any guest, any day of the week. This dish is great whether you eat it straight out of the oven or as leftovers that have chilled overnight. Simply reheat leftovers in the microwave covered by a damp paper towel and voilà—a meal in a pinch (and the longer it sits, the better it gets!). I love cooking for tomorrow *today*. This dish is versatile and, when paired with a salad, can even stand alone as a main dish for a fun lunch, brunch, or dinner option. Ain't no shame in a dinner egg game!

Preheat the oven to 350°F. Grease an 8-inch square baking dish.

In a large sauté pan, melt the butter over medium-high heat. Add the onion, mushrooms, celery, and scallions and cook, stirring occasionally, until the onion is translucent and soft, 4 to 5 minutes. Add ¼ teaspoon of the salt, the sausage, and the spinach and sauté until the spinach has wilted and started to cook, about 1 minute. Turn the heat off and stir in ½ cup of the corn, the basil, and the parsley. Set aside.

In a blender or food processor, combine the remaining ¾ cup corn, the eggs, half-and-half, pepper, remaining ½ teaspoon salt, and the sage and puree until the mixture is smooth.

MAKES 8 SERVINGS

2 tablespoons butter, plus more for greasing

½ cup diced onion

½ cup diced mushrooms

¼ cup diced celery

¼ cup chopped scallions

¾ teaspoon salt

6 turkey breakfast sausage patties, diced

2 large handfuls of baby spinach

1¼ cups frozen corn kernels, thawed

2 tablespoons chopped fresh basil

1 tablespoon chopped fresh parsley, plus more for garnishing

10 large eggs

¾ cup half-and-half

¼ teaspoon ground black pepper

1 teaspoon dried sage

12 King's Hawaiian original sweet rolls, torn into chunks

2 cups shredded cheddar cheese

continued

ryan's all-in-one savory breakfast bake, continued

In a large bowl, combine the torn rolls, corn mixture, half the cheese, and the sautéed veggies and turkey. Pour the mixture into the prepared baking dish and cover with aluminum foil. Bake for 30 minutes, then remove the foil, sprinkle the remaining cheese over the top of the casserole, and bake until the cheese is bubbly and beginning to brown, about 30 minutes. Let rest for at least 10 minutes. Garnish with parsley before serving.

Notes

- If you like your bread pudding a little crustier, try using artisan sourdough bread instead of the Hawaiian rolls, and bake the casserole in a 9 x 13-inch pan. It will cook a little faster, and the tops and edges will be crunchier.

- You can use any fillings you like, but my favorite is turkey sausage, and I always try to sneak in green veggies whenever I can.

candied bacon breakfast wellingtons

Prep Time: 20 minutes | Cook Time: 25 to 30 minutes

MAKES 8 SERVINGS

½ cup lightly packed brown sugar

1 tablespoon chili powder

¼ teaspoon plus ⅛ teaspoon ground black pepper

12 slices thick-cut bacon

8 large eggs, beaten, plus 1 egg yolk for the egg wash

3 tablespoons chopped fresh chives

1 tablespoon milk

¼ teaspoon salt

Cooking spray

½ (8-ounce) package cream cheese, at room temperature

¼ teaspoon minced garlic

¼ teaspoon Old Bay seasoning

1 (17-ounce) package frozen puff pastry (2 sheets), thawed in the fridge

¼ cup salt-free everything bagel seasoning

Not only do I cook for my wife and daughter on a daily basis, I also find myself (very) frequently cooking for guests who are staying at our unofficial "Scott Family Bed-and-Breakfast." There is hardly a time at Casa de Scott when someone is not residing in our guest bedroom. What can I say—we love having our friends and family around us. Look, if I can have food that is already prepared and that only needs to be reheated, I am *all* about it. Enter these Candied Bacon Breakfast Wellingtons. I am a fan of semi-homemade products that can make life easier. Puff pastry dough is one of those cheater products that is worth its weight in gold for its time-saving powers.

Feel free to use this recipe as a guide and then adapt it for your preferences. For example, add roasted eggplant and mozzarella for an Italian flair; or switch out the bacon for turkey sausage and add bell pepper, jalapeños, and cheddar cheese for a more southwestern angle. Freeze this dish for any time a quick draw is needed in the feed-your-guests-some-breakfast department, and you will absolutely be the host/hostess with the most-est. Now there will be even *more* time for mimosas and Bloody Marys!

Preheat the oven to 350°F. Line a baking sheet with aluminum foil or parchment paper.

In a small bowl, mix the brown sugar, chili powder, and ¼ teaspoon of the pepper. Arrange the bacon on the prepared baking sheet and top the bacon slices with half the brown sugar mixture. Use the back of a spoon to press the sugar into the bacon and spread it evenly. Flip the bacon slices and repeat on the other side with the rest of the sugar mixture. Bake the sugared bacon until browned and the edges have crisped from the caramelized sugar, 12 to 15 minutes. Set the bacon aside to cool.

Heat a large nonstick skillet over medium-low heat. In a small bowl, whisk together the beaten eggs, chives, milk, salt, and remaining ⅛ teaspoon pepper. When the pan is hot, spray it with cooking spray and pour in the egg mixture. Swirl the pan so the eggs coat the entire bottom of the pan. Cover the pan and cook over low heat until the egg is just cooked and no longer wet on top, 3 to 4 minutes. Remove the pan from the heat and set aside to cool.

In a small bowl, mix the cream cheese, garlic, and Old Bay.

In a separate small bowl, beat the egg yolk with 2 tablespoons water to make an egg wash.

Grease a baking sheet with butter or cooking spray. Unfold the thawed puff pastry sheets and lay both sheets flat on the counter with one long side facing you. Spread the cream cheese mixture over both sheets of puff pastry. Cut the cooled omelet in half and put one half on each puff pastry rectangle on top of the cream cheese, about 1 inch from the edge. Arrange the cooled candied bacon on top of the omelet. Fold up the bottom edge of each puff pastry sheet to cover the fillings, then continue rolling it up until you get to the end. Brush the edge of the pastry with egg wash and seal it up, keeping the seam on the bottom of the roll. Brush both rolls with the egg wash and sprinkle the tops with the everything bagel seasoning. Using a sharp knife, cut each roll crosswise into 4 pieces. Place them seam-side down on the prepared baking sheet, spacing them 2 to 3 inches apart. Bake for 25 to 30 minutes, until the Wellingtons are puffy and golden brown and the cream cheese is bubbling out of the sides. These are great served hot from the oven or cooled to room temperature.

Notes

★ After filling and rolling the Wellingtons, you can wrap them in plastic wrap and refrigerate for up to 24 hours or freeze them for up to 1 month. When baking frozen Wellingtons, be sure to thaw them in the fridge overnight, then bake as directed.

★ Be sure to use a salt-free everything bagel seasoning; the salted version is way too salty for this recipe. If you like, you can use just sesame seeds or poppy seeds instead, or skip the topping altogether.

twice-baked denver-style stuffed sweet potatoes

Prep Time: 10 minutes | Cook Time: 15 minutes

MAKES 4 SERVINGS

4 small sweet potatoes or yams, scrubbed

4 tablespoons (½ stick) unsalted butter, at room temperature

2 teaspoons real maple syrup

½ teaspoon kosher salt

2 tablespoons olive oil

½ cup diced red onion (½ large)

1 cup diced bell pepper (1 medium)

½ cup diced mushrooms (2 ounces)

½ cup diced cooked ham

6 large eggs

2 tablespoons half-and-half or milk

¾ cup shredded cheddar cheese

2 tablespoons chopped fresh chives or parsley, for garnish

When I was between the ages of eleven and thirteen, my parents owned a little diner in Los Banos, California, called Chubby's. One of the first short-order dishes I learned to cook was a Denver scramble. I was a proud (and painfully awkward) prepubescent chef in a little white apron and paper hat. Can we all picture that? Now, in an attempt to avoid serving panfried or crispy hash brown–style potatoes with every breakfast dish that I make at home, I created *this* glorious concoction—and Olive definitely approves. She has always loved sweet potatoes; as a baby, she went bonkers for sweet potato puree, and her love affair continues! This recipe came from a morning mash-up of a little bit of this and a little bit of that, with a nod to both Chubby's Diner and my sweet potato–obsessed offspring.

Preheat the oven to 375°F. Line a baking sheet with aluminum foil.

Prepare the sweet potatoes. You can do it the old-fashioned way by wrapping each potato in foil and baking at 375°F for an hour, or you can do it the busy dad way and pierce each potato 3 or 4 times per side, and microwave on high for 3 minutes. Flip them over and nuke them until they are soft when you squeeze them, about 3 minutes more, and you have "baked" potatoes in just 6 minutes.

Meanwhile, in a small bowl, stir together the butter, maple syrup, and ¼ teaspoon of the salt until fully combined.

Make a slit down the center of each sweet potato and fluff the inside with a fork. Divide the maple butter evenly among the potatoes and spread it around the insides. Set the buttered potatoes aside on the prepared baking sheet while you prepare the filling.

In a large pan, heat the olive oil over medium heat. Add the onion, bell pepper, and mushrooms and sauté, stirring occasionally, until the vegetables have softened and the onion becomes translucent, about 5 minutes. Add the ham and sauté until the meat is heated through, about 2 minutes.

In a small bowl, beat the eggs, half-and-half, and remaining ¼ teaspoon salt. Add the egg mixture to the pan with the vegetables and ham and cook over low-medium heat, stirring continuously, for 2 to 3 minutes, until the scramble is almost cooked through (you should still see some streaks of uncooked egg). Remove from the heat.

Divide the scrambled egg mixture among the buttered potatoes, mounding the filling up with a spoon. Top each potato with a generous amount of cheese and bake the filled potatoes until the cheese is bubbling and melted, 10 to 15 minutes. Garnish with chopped chives or parsley and serve immediately.

Notes

⭐ If you're not a sweet potato fan, substitute russets or Yukon golds. You can also substitute whatever veggies and meats you like in the scramble: cooked bacon and onions, breakfast sausage and sage—the possibilities are endless!

⭐ This recipe is a favorite for dinner at my house. Who says eggs have to be for breakfast?

old-school spiced pork hash with potatoes, herbs, and worcestershire

Prep Time: 20 minutes | Cook Time: 15 minutes for the hash cakes; 6 hours for roasting | Inactive Time: 8+ hours for marinating, plus the roasting time

People always talk about the location of their first date. My wife and I don't only have *one* location that holds that title, but instead, four! Yep, we went to *four* places on our first date (I was trying really hard to impress her). We followed up that epic four-destination date with five more dates in a row, so our first date was clearly a success! Ninety days later, we moved in together, and the rest is history. As much as I would love to give my tight pants and good hair the credit, it was actually me making *this* dish that sealed the deal, and I'm pretty sure the pork hash is at least 50 percent of the reason my wife agreed to marry me. In my extensive culinary arsenal, there is no other dish she requests more often than this one! Despite it being incredible (and a good way to catch a spouse), it does take a bit of time to make, so plan ahead; you can even make it ahead and freeze it. Serve these heavenly breakfast cakes with fried or poached eggs. They are a winner for any family meal or a hot date. Warning: This hash may fast-track your relationship, so be careful who you serve it to!

COOK THE PORK: Line a baking sheet with parchment paper or aluminum foil.

Rinse the pork butt under cold tap water and pat dry with paper towels. Put the pork on the prepared baking sheet and completely coat it with the spice rub, making sure the whole piece of meat is coated with spices. Wrap the meat in plastic wrap or put it in a large zip-top bag and refrigerate overnight or for at least 8 hours.

When you're ready to cook the pork, preheat the oven to 325°F. Take the pork out of the fridge, unwrap it, and let it rest at room temperature.

MAKES 15 CAKES

For the pork
1 (5-pound) bone-in pork butt/shoulder

⅓ cup Spice Rub (recipe follows)

1 cup chicken broth

For the hash
2 tablespoons olive oil

1 large onion, diced (about 2 cups)

2 large Yukon gold potatoes, diced (about 4 cups)

3 teaspoons kosher salt

½ bunch parsley, coarsely chopped (about ½ cup)

2 tablespoons Worcestershire sauce

1 tablespoon Spice Rub (recipe follows)

1 teaspoon ground black pepper

1 teaspoon Lawry's Seasoned Salt

6 dashes of Tabasco sauce

4 tablespoons olive oil, for frying the cakes

continued

old-school spiced pork hash with potatoes, herbs, and worcestershire, continued

In a large casserole or Dutch oven with a lid, bring the broth to a boil, then turn the heat off and carefully place the pork in the hot broth. Put the lid on, transfer the pot to the oven, and roast the pork for 6 hours, until tender and falling apart. Remove the pork from the broth and pull the meat into chunks. Put half of the meat in the bowl of a stand mixer; transfer the rest to a zip-top bag, flattening it out for easy storage and defrosting, and store it in the freezer for later use.

MAKE THE HASH: In a large sauté pan, heat the olive oil over medium-high heat. Add the onion and cook, stirring frequently, for 4 to 5 minutes, until translucent. Add the cooked onion to the pork in the bowl.

Rinse the potatoes with cold water, put them in a large pot and add enough cold water to cover them by 2 inches. Bring the pot to a boil over high heat, then add 1 teaspoon of the salt. Reduce the heat to medium-low and simmer the potatoes, uncovered, until they are almost fork-tender, about 15 minutes. Drain the cooked potatoes and add them to the bowl with the pork and onion.

Add the parsley, Worcestershire, spice rub, pepper, Lawry's, Tabasco, and remaining 2 teaspoons salt to the bowl. Put the bowl on the mixer fitted with the paddle attachment and mix on low speed until the pork breaks up completely and the mixture looks almost smooth, about 2 minutes. There should still be some small chunks of potato, but the pork will look almost like a pâté. If you don't have a stand mixer, you can mix it by hand with a wooden spoon (you will have to really put some muscle into it and it will take 5 to 6 minutes to fully break down and become as creamy as it should be).

Heat a large skillet or griddle over medium-high heat. Pour 2 tablespoons of the olive oil onto the hot skillet and swirl it around to coat the pan. Carefully drop ⅓-cup portions of the hash mixture onto the pan, flattening them with a spatula as you add them. Cook until well browned on one side, about 2 minutes, then flip and cook for 2 minutes more on the second side. Transfer the hash cakes to a plate and repeat to cook the remaining hash cakes in batches, adding more oil to the pan by the tablespoon when it starts looking dry. Serve immediately.

Notes

* This recipe makes twice the amount of pork and way more spice rub than you actually need. I wrote it that way because, after roasting, I freeze half the meat! I know that making this dish from scratch takes some planning ahead and a couple of days (believe me—it is worth it), but sometimes Lesley gets a craving for it and I don't have time to marinate and roast a whole pork butt. That's when the leftover roasted pork comes in handy. I freeze it flat in zip-top bags so it defrosts quickly and we can have this amazing hash after a quick defrost in the microwave.

* I use the spice rub as a seasoning salt on so many things, such as grilled steaks, sautéed mushrooms, and roasted whole chicken, and I just love having it in the pantry ready to go.

* I simmer my potatoes on medium-low heat instead of rapidly boiling them because I find that boiling tears the skins up and quickly creates a soggy, mushy mess in the water. I want my potatoes to have bite and body, not to become watery potato soup.

* You can also freeze the hash mixture to cook it later. Thaw the bag of frozen hash mixture in the fridge or at room temperature, then scoop and fry the cakes as directed in the recipe.

Spice Rub

MAKES 1½ CUPS

½ cup kosher salt

5 tablespoons dried thyme

3 tablespoons ground coriander

3 tablespoons ground cumin

3 tablespoons ground allspice

1 tablespoon ground nutmeg

1 tablespoon ground black pepper

1 tablespoon ground ginger

1 tablespoon garlic powder

In a small bowl, whisk together all the ingredients to combine. Store the spice rub in an airtight container at room temperature for up to 1 year.

banana, brown butter granola, and yogurt mash-up

Prep Time: 15 minutes | Cook Time: 20 minutes

MAKES 4 SERVINGS

3 ripe or overripe bananas

1 tablespoon chia seeds

2 cups plain Greek yogurt

¾ cup Brown Butter Granola (recipe follows)

2 tablespoons dried cranberries

¼ cup freeze-dried raspberries or strawberries

2 tablespoons roasted salted pepitas (hulled pumpkin seeds)

¼ cup pomegranate seeds

You can only make so many pancakes with overripe bananas before your start to go cross-eyed. This recipe was created on a whim when I was desperate to figure out more ways to use up the overripe bananas lurking at the bottom of my fruit basket. You can customize it any way you like. No seeds in the house? No problem! Do you have fresh berries instead of freeze-dried? Please proceed! If you use cashew or almond yogurt and omit the honey from the granola (or substitute agave syrup), this can be a vegan dish. The flavor profile can be changed throughout the year to accommodate seasonal ingredients, so feel free to mix it up and be creative. You really cannot go wrong. I like building this in a clear glass pie dish to really showcase all the layers. Olive gets a kick out of seeing what new and fun things I've included each time I serve this to her. (She also loves to help dish it up, so I always have plenty of napkins nearby.) This is fast to assemble and basically foolproof. Give it a whirl!

Smash the peeled bananas with a fork in the bottom of a large platter or pie dish. Sprinkle the chia seeds evenly over the bananas, then add the yogurt, spreading it evenly to cover the bananas. Sprinkle the granola and cranberries evenly over the yogurt, then top with the freeze-dried berries, pepitas, and pomegranate seeds. Serve immediately, or cover and refrigerate until serving time, up to 4 hours.

Notes

⭐ If you plan to serve the mash-up later, be sure you have covered the banana layer fully with the yogurt to avoid browning.

⭐ The ripe bananas should be sweet enough to flavor the parfait perfectly, but if you prefer it a little sweeter or have to use slightly under ripe bananas, just drizzle the parfait with honey or agave.

Brown Butter Granola

MAKES 3¼ CUPS

8 tablespoons (1 stick) unsalted butter

¼ cup honey

2½ cups rolled oats

¼ cup flaxseeds

½ cup unsweetened coconut flakes

1 teaspoon vanilla extract

½ teaspoon ground ginger

½ teaspoon ground cinnamon

Pinch of salt

Preheat the oven to 300°F. Line a baking sheet with parchment paper.

In a small saucepan, melt the butter over low heat, then cook until the bottom starts to turn brown, 4 to 5 minutes. Immediately pour the browned butter into a medium bowl and add the honey. Whisk to combine and melt the honey. Add the remaining ingredients and stir until well combined.

Pour the granola onto the prepared baking sheet and spread it into a thin, even layer. Bake for 15 minutes, then remove from the oven and carefully stir with a wooden spoon or spatula. Return the pan to the oven and bake until the granola is evenly browned, about 7 minutes more. Set aside to cool. Store the granola in an airtight container at room temperature for up to 2 weeks.

on-the-go "green monster" frittata bites

Prep Time: 10 minutes | Cook Time: 20 minutes

It's really funny (and sad), but chefs typically go the entire day without eating (just ask a chef's husband or wife). We come straight home from a fourteen-hour workday and raid the fridge. My days of working in restaurants were also my days of drinking (copious amounts of) green smoothies. They were a fast and portable way to get a meal in my loudly growling stomach during a hectic workday. Green smoothies are super-healthy, and I fully support the continuing trend, but I really started to miss the act of *chewing!* This recipe is my version of a green powerhouse breakfast (or any meal), and it's one you can actually sink your teeth into. It's basically a superfood frittata baked in a muffin tin. I love being able to source much-needed energy from eggs, flax, and chard. These mini-frittatas are portable, perfectly portioned, and easy to grab on your way out the door when you're in a hurry. I often pack these to bring with me on my flights to tame the "snacking monster" within (instead of gorging on airport food and airplane snacks). To mix it up a bit, you can top them with soft goat cheese, or chop one up and enjoy it as a modern version of egg salad. Put turkey bacon or sausage in the recipe, and you can increase the protein even more. Pack them for lunches at the office, pop them in your child's lunch box for school, or bring them on a road trip to avoid the fast-food hustle.

Preheat the oven to 350°F. Spray a standard nonstick muffin tin with cooking spray.

Rinse the shredded potato in a sieve and squeeze all the moisture out by hand. Set aside.

MAKES 12 MINI-FRITTATAS

Cooking spray

1 cup fresh or frozen shredded russet potato

2 tablespoons butter

½ cup diced onion

1 garlic clove, minced (about 1 teaspoon)

1 bunch of Swiss chard, stemmed and finely chopped

7 large eggs

¾ cup plain Greek yogurt

1 tablespoon flaxseeds

¼ teaspoon salt

3 or 4 large fresh basil leaves

½ teaspoon chopped fresh rosemary leaves

½ cup loosely packed fresh parsley leaves

1 tablespoon chopped fresh chives

1 cup shredded Swiss cheese

continued

In a large sauté pan, melt the butter over medium-high heat. Add the onion, potato, and garlic. Cook, stirring occasionally, until the onion is soft and the potato starts to color, 4 to 5 minutes. Add the chard and sauté until wilted, about 1 minute. Remove from the heat and set aside.

In a blender, combine the eggs, yogurt, flaxseeds, salt, basil, rosemary, parsley, and chives and pulse until the mixture is smooth and green.

Divide the vegetable mixture among the wells of the prepared muffin tin, filling each about halfway. Pour the egg mixture on top of the vegetables, filling each muffin cup about three-quarters full. Give the contents of each well a quick stir to make sure the egg and veggies are properly mixed up.

Bake until the egg is completely set and no longer wet on top, 12 to 15 minutes, then carefully remove the pan from the oven and sprinkle each mini-frittata with about 2 tablespoons of the cheese. Bake for 3 minutes more to melt the cheese, then remove from the oven.

You can serve the frittatas hot from the oven, but they are also amazing (and so portable!) at room temperature.

Notes

★ Flaxseeds add even more protein and nutrients to this healthy breakfast—don't skip them!

★ Try these as the filling for a breakfast burrito or pita, or just eat one out of hand like a muffin when you're on the go.

no-knead diy english muffins

Prep Time: 25 minutes | Cook Time: 20 minutes | Inactive Time: 8+ hours

Sometimes big life decisions have small (and goofy) reasons behind them. One silly influence behind my decision to go to culinary school was a simple kitchen aroma: the scent of English muffins searing on a griddle. Trust me, if you don't have the patience to bake, this no-knead English muffin recipe is a great starter bread for you! English muffins can find a place on your plate at any meal. You can swap it in for your breakfast biscuit, your white bread for a turkey sandwich, or your hamburger bun to hold that juicy bacon cheeseburger. Not only that, but they freeze really well. They've become a *necessity* in our home, and soon they'll be a staple in yours, too.

In a small saucepan, heat the milk and 1 cup of water over low heat to just above lukewarm, then pour the liquid into a large bowl (alternatively, warm them in the microwave). Stir in the yeast and sugar. Add the all-purpose flour, whole wheat flour, and salt. Stir until the flour is completely hydrated and the dough has become a sticky mass. Cover the bowl loosely (you can just throw a kitchen towel over it) and let it rest at room temperature for about 20 minutes.

Using a rubber spatula, scrape the sides of the bowl thoroughly and mix the dough with a wooden spoon for 3 to 4 minutes. It will get pretty stiff and thick, but just keep mixing to help develop the dough's structure.

Grease a large container or bowl (at least twice as large as the dough) with cooking spray or vegetable oil and pour the dough into it. Cover with a lid or plastic wrap and refrigerate overnight. The dough needs to ferment in the fridge for at least 8 hours, but should not be held for longer than 24 hours or the yeast will no longer be active.

The next day, generously sprinkle a baking sheet with cornmeal (use more cornmeal than you think you'll need—there's nothing worse than dough sticking to the baking sheet when you try to move it). Turn the cold dough out onto a heavily floured countertop. Sprinkle more flour on top of the dough and gently stretch and push the dough into a large round, 1 to 1½ inches thick. Using the rim

continued

MAKES 16 ENGLISH MUFFINS

1 cup milk

1 (¼-ounce) packet instant yeast (2¼ teaspoons)

1 tablespoon sugar

3½ cups all-purpose flour, plus 1 to 2 cups for dusting

1 cup whole wheat flour

1 tablespoon plus 2 teaspoons salt

Cooking spray or vegetable oil, for greasing (optional)

1 cup cornmeal, for dusting

¼ cup vegetable oil, for frying

of a drinking glass or a 3-inch cookie cutter, cut out rounds of the dough, keeping them close together to avoid wasting dough and dipping the glass or cutter in flour after each cut. Use a spatula to transfer the muffins to the baking sheet. Sprinkle more cornmeal on top of the English muffins and cover with a clean kitchen towel. Set the baking sheet in a warm spot in your kitchen and let the muffins rise until they puff up by about 50 percent, 30 to 35 minutes.

Heat a large griddle or skillet over medium-low heat. Pour a couple of tablespoons of vegetable oil into the hot pan. Using a spatula, gently transfer the muffins to the pan, spacing them about an inch apart. Once the pan is filled, cover it with a lid (if using a griddle, cover with an upside-down cake pan) and cook until the muffins are browned on one side, about 2 minutes. Flip the muffins, cover, and cook for 2 minutes more. Once the muffins are out of the pan, give it a quick wipe with a paper towel and repeat to cook the remaining muffins, using new oil for each batch. Let the English muffins cool completely before slicing them in half. Enjoy them soft and fresh with salted butter and jam (try the jam on page 31) or toasted up for my family's favorite breakfast sandwiches (page 28).

Notes

* The overnight cold fermentation of this dough makes it possible to mix by hand, and also helps to achieve a super-delicious, complex flavor along with those amazing nooks and crannies. Just be sure not to manhandle the dough or press it down when rolling it out; that's a surefire way to destroy any bubbles you've developed in the dough.

* Try using sesame or poppy seeds instead of cornmeal to coat the English muffins; the seeds toast up while the dough cooks and create an awesome crunchy crust.

* Don't reroll the dough scraps to make more English muffins; they will be too doughy and won't have the nooks and crannies. Instead, toss the dough in cinnamon and brown sugar, press into a loaf or small cake pan, and bake at 350°F for 30 minutes. Drizzle a little vanilla icing over the top and you have . . . monkey bread!

no-bake blueberry energy bites

Prep Time: 5 minutes | Cook Time: 0

Since my wife, Lesley, travels a lot and is perpetually in motion, energy bars are her lifeline in a too-busy-for-a-sit-down-meal world. But although store-bought energy bars serve their purpose, they are pricey, and also include some ingredients that I would prefer to avoid. Instead of continually restocking Lesley's stash, I came up with a tasty homemade solution packed with protein and fiber. When I was working out the recipe for these no-bake energy bites, I wanted to be sure they were healthy and substantial but wouldn't leave you feeling weighed down. These are kid-friendly and make a fun finger food for toddlers and adults alike.

In a blender, grind the flaxseeds to a coarse powder. Transfer the ground flaxseeds to a food processor and add the cashews, oats, blueberries, agave, salt, dates, figs, lemon zest, and lemon juice. Process until the mixture becomes cohesive and forms a ball when pressed together, about 1 minute. The nuts should be broken into small chunks and the dates and figs should be fully pulverized.

Using a teaspoon or melon baller, scoop the mixture into evenly sized balls, 1 to 2 inches in diameter. Roll the balls in your hands to make them round, then roll them in either sunflower seeds or chocolate chips to coat. Store the energy bites in an airtight container at room temperature for up to 4 days.

MAKES 16 TO 18 BITES

2 tablespoons flaxseeds

½ cup raw cashews

¼ cup quick-cooking or rolled oats

½ cup dried blueberries

1 tablespoon agave syrup or honey

⅛ teaspoon salt

¼ cup stemmed and pitted dates

¼ cup stemmed dried figs

1 teaspoon grated lemon zest

½ teaspoon fresh lemon juice

1 cup toasted sunflower seeds or mini chocolate chips, for rolling

Notes

* If your food processor has very sharp blades and has less than a 7-cup capacity, you may be able to use it for grinding the flaxseeds instead of using a blender. A larger food processor will just fling the seeds around without grinding them.

* For texture and shelf stability, always use dried fruit. You can control the sweetness by adjusting the amount of agave, and you can change the kind of nut or other ingredients you use for rolling. But figs and dates are important for binding the ingredients.

scott family tree egg sandos

Prep Time: 5 minutes | Cook Time: 5 minutes

MAKES 4 SERVINGS

Canola oil, vegetable oil, or other neutral-tasting oil, for frying

4 eggs

Salt and ground black pepper

4 English muffins, halved

4 slices cheese

4 teaspoons mayonnaise

Additional toppings, as desired (see page 30)

There are a lot of gadgets out there that claim to make the perfect egg, but all you really need is a no-frills 8-inch nonstick skillet. Trust me, leave the spatula in the drawer; all it takes is a little flick of the wrist to flip an egg. It may seem difficult at first, but with a little practice, you'll be mistaken for a line cook in no time. Start by practicing with ½ cup of dried beans in the pan. Gently flick your wrist to toss the beans without scattering them on the floor. Once you've mastered the beans, it's time to graduate to a piece of dry toast, using the same motion to flip the bread. Wasn't that easy? Now you're ready to proceed.

In our home, egg sandos are a way of life (and not just for breakfast). Something fun about this approach to creating egg sandwiches is that each person is able to build their own version with all of *their* favorite additions. Lesley, Olive, and I all have very different ways that we like to make them. As with most toddlers, Olive's tastes change about every half hour, and depending on the rest of our moods, so does my taste and Lesley's, too. These egg sandwiches are easy to make and nearly foolproof, because they're made exactly as *you* like them! Using homemade English muffins (see page 23) will take things up a notch for the best egg sandwich you've ever eaten!

Heat an 8-inch nonstick skillet over medium-high heat. Brush the skillet with oil. (You don't need a lot of oil, just enough to get the egg sizzling.) Crack an egg into the skillet and season with salt and pepper. Cook the egg without disturbing it. Here's the secret: You want to cook the egg about three-quarters of the way through. The egg white should be almost completely cooked, with just the portion closest to the yolk still not set. Give the pan a gentle swirl to loosen the egg and then, just like we practiced, flip that egg!

continued

Scott Family Favorite Toppings

Ryan's Sando
Medium-cooked egg

4 slices crispy bacon

2 slices sharp cheddar cheese

¼ avocado

2 tablespoons hot sauce
(I prefer Crystal brand)

Lesley's Sando
Over-easy egg

½ cup fresh baby spinach

1 slice Swiss cheese

Olive's Sando
Fried egg

¼ avocado

1 slice honey ham

1 slice cheddar cheese

For a Soft or Over-Easy Egg: Remove the skillet from the heat and let sit for 10 seconds (just long enough to finish cooking the egg white) before sliding the egg onto a plate.

For a Medium-Cooked Egg: Cook over medium-high heat for 30 seconds more before sliding the egg onto a plate.

For a Hard-Cooked Egg: Cook over medium-high heat for 1 to 1½ minutes, until the yolk is firm to the touch, before sliding the egg onto a plate.

Toast the English muffins. While they are still warm, place the cheese on the split side of the top halves. Cover with a bowl and allow the heat from the muffins to melt the cheese (or pop them into a warm oven).

Smear the bottom halves of the English muffins with the mayonnaise. Top each with an egg and everyone's favorite toppings, then close the sandwiches with the top halves of the muffins.

Notes

★ Serve immediately or wrap in parchment and take it on-the-go. The cheese will continue to melt as it sits in its warm cocoon of hot fried egg and toasted English muffin all wrapped up in parchment. By the time you open it at work, school, or in the car, it will be perfect.

yeasted buttermilk biscuits with almost-no-sugar strawberry jam

Prep Time: 5 minutes | Cook Time: 15 to 17 minutes

If you've ever seen me at live cooking demos, you've probably also heard me talk about my grandma's biscuit recipe. All of my childhood, I was so in love with the buttery little mounds of magic that she created! When I was asked to feature my favorite childhood recipe in a magazine after I was on *Top Chef,* I instantly knew what recipe I wanted to use. I called Grandma Lena and told her that a famous magazine wanted to feature her biscuit recipe, and I asked if she would share it with me. I'll never forget her reply: "Sure, honey. Just cut the recipe off the back of the Bisquick box and give them that." I'm pretty sure that all the magic and mystery of my childhood was shattered in that one honest moment! My grandma was the best. She seemed larger than life, and there was absolutely *no* shame in her game! She wore her nightdress 24/7 and *rocked* the look. So, in honor of her authenticity, I created this really great recipe for buttermilk biscuits, which are definitely even a notch above Grandma's biscuits (yes, the ones that fooled me for years!). I've put my own spin on these by making the biscuits with yeast and baking powder (which gives them a more complex flavor and a bit more fluffiness). Enjoy . . . possibly in your pj's. I hope I've made my grandma proud.

MAKES 16 BISCUITS

4½ cups all-purpose flour

3 tablespoons plus 1 teaspoon baking powder

1 teaspoon kosher salt

9 ounces (2⅛ sticks) cold butter, cubed, plus 2 tablespoons (¼ stick), melted

1½ cups buttermilk

2 tablespoons honey

1 egg

1 teaspoon instant yeast

1 tablespoon Maldon sea salt

Preheat the oven to 375°F. Line an 8-inch square baking dish with plastic wrap.

In a large bowl, combine the flour, baking powder, and salt. Add the cold butter cubes and quickly work in the butter with a pastry cutter or your hands until it is broken down into lima bean–size pieces. Put the bowl in the fridge while you gather the wet ingredients.

continued

In a large measuring cup, whisk together the buttermilk, honey, egg, and yeast. Add the buttermilk mixture to the butter-flour mixture and stir with a wooden spoon just until the dough becomes a shaggy mass. Using your hands, press the dough together and mix in the bowl until it forms a shaggy ball. There should still be some dry bits at the bottom of the bowl.

Press the dough into the prepared baking dish. Flip the baking dish over, remove the plastic, and pat the dough out into a square about 1 inch thick. Cut the dough into 4 strips, then cut those strips into 4 squares each, making a total of 16 biscuits. Place the biscuits 2 inches apart on two baking sheets and bake until golden brown, about 15 minutes. Gently open a biscuit to make sure the center is cooked; if it is still a little doughy, bake for 2 to 3 minutes more then check again.

Remove from the oven. While the biscuits are hot from the oven, brush them with the melted butter and sprinkle a pinch of Maldon salt on each one, then serve.

Almost-No-Sugar Strawberry Jam

Prep Time: 5 minutes | Cook Time: 30 minutes

MAKES 1 PINT

4 cups frozen whole strawberries

¼ cup apple juice

2 tablespoons sugar

1½ tablespoons powdered pectin

1 tablespoon balsamic vinegar or lemon juice

¼ teaspoon ground black pepper

continued

Preheat the oven to 300°F for sterilizing the jars.

In a medium saucepan, combine all the ingredients. Cook over low heat, stirring frequently, until the strawberries are completely thawed, about 5 minutes. Increase the heat to medium and simmer the jam, stirring frequently, for 30 minutes. The strawberries should have mostly broken down at this point and the jam should be thickened (it will thicken more as it cools).

Meanwhile, to sterilize the jars, clean them with warm soapy water and rinse thoroughly. Put the jars in a baking dish in the oven while the jam is cooking. When the jam is finished, carefully pull the jars out of the oven. Very carefully pour the hot jam into the hot jars, leaving ½ inch of headspace, and put the lids on. Leave the jam at room temperature to cool for at least 6 hours or overnight. The gradual cooling of the jam and jars will create a vacuum and seal the jars airtight.

Because of the small percentage of sugar and the relatively short cooking time, as well as not being boiled in the jar, this jam will not keep as long as a traditional jam or preserve and should not be stored at room temperature. Store it in the fridge and use within 4 weeks.

Notes

★ Since this jam has little sugar plus additions of balsamic and black pepper, it's great in both sweet and savory applications. Try it with fancy cheese (or on a block of cream cheese!) and spiced nuts.

★ Don't have buttermilk for the biscuits? No problem! I often make sour milk to replace buttermilk in recipes. Use this ratio: 1 cup milk to 1 tablespoon vinegar. Almost any vinegar will do, just be aware that rice vinegar is sweet and balsamic vinegar is brown, so those might not be the best choices.

grapefruit poppy seed pound cake

Prep Time: 10 minutes | Cook Time: 1 hour

In my early years growing up in California, we lived in Oakhurst, where my parents worked at a five-diamond resort. I was in awe of the "brûleéd" roasted grapefruit that they would prepare. It could not have been simpler (or more impressive in taste). It really was just half a grapefruit with turbinado sugar sprinkled on top, then broiled until the surface was caramelized and crunchy like the top of a crème brûleé. I *love* taking favorite food memories from my childhood and creating new adaptations. The way I see it, every recipe has some kind of origin story. Passing on these stories in the form of recipes feels pretty great. In this particular recipe, I give a nod to that special grapefruit dish of my childhood by using grapefruit instead of lemons in a pound cake, topping it with a sweet, citrusy grapefruit glaze. This cake goes well with cheese boards, breakfast, or brunch with friends. Enjoy it as a special dessert on your birthday or take it to a work party and watch your coworkers swarm.

MAKE THE CAKE: Preheat the oven to 350°F. Grease a 9 x 5-inch loaf pan with cooking spray or brush the sides and bottom with vegetable oil.

Sift together the flour, baking powder, baking soda, salt, and poppy seeds into a medium bowl. (If the poppy seeds don't go through the strainer, just add them after sifting the rest of the dry ingredients.)

In a small bowl, whisk together the sour cream, grapefruit zest, grapefruit juice, lemon zest, lemon juice, and vanilla.

In a large bowl using an electric mixer, cream the butter, coconut oil, granulated sugar, and brown sugar until light and fluffy, 3 to 4 minutes. Add the eggs one at a time, being sure to mix thoroughly after each addition before adding the next.

MAKES ONE 9 X 5-INCH LOAF

For the cake

Cooking spray or vegetable oil, for greasing

2 cups all-purpose flour

1½ teaspoons baking powder

¼ teaspoon baking soda

1 teaspoon salt

2 tablespoons poppy seeds

½ cup sour cream

2 tablespoons grated grapefruit zest

¼ cup fresh grapefruit juice

1 tablespoon grated lemon zest

2 tablespoons fresh lemon juice

1 tablespoon vanilla extract

8 tablespoons (1 stick) unsalted butter, at room temperature

½ cup coconut oil, at room temperature

1¼ cups granulated sugar

¼ cup brown sugar, lightly packed

3 large eggs, at room temperature

continued

grapefruit poppy seed pound cake, continued

For the sugar glaze

1 cup confectioners' sugar

2 tablespoons fresh grapefruit juice

Pinch of salt

Add the flour mixture and juice mixture alternately, starting and ending with the flour mixture and stopping to scrape the sides of the bowl after each addition to ensure even mixing. When the last of the ingredients has been added, give the bowl one final scrape and mix the batter for another minute.

Pour the batter into the prepared loaf pan and use the back of a spoon to smooth and flatten out the top.

Bake the loaf until the top springs back to the touch and a toothpick inserted into the center comes out with just a couple of moist crumbs clinging to it, about 1 hour.

MAKE THE GLAZE: In a small cup or bowl, mix the confectioners' sugar, grapefruit juice, and salt until smooth.

While the loaf is still hot, gently run a knife around the sides of the loaf and turn it out onto a wire rack set over a baking sheet. Be careful—the cake will be a little fragile. Using a spoon, drizzle the icing over the top of the loaf, letting it drip down the sides. Let the cake cool to room temperature (if you can!) before slicing and enjoying it. Citrus pound cakes are always tastier the next day: Wrap it tightly in plastic wrap once it is cool and store at room temperature for 3 to 4 days. (You can do the same with any leftovers.)

Note

★ Don't like grapefruit? Use orange, lime, or Meyer lemon! The cake base is so moist and versatile, you can use virtually any citrus. If you use a sweet citrus like orange, reduce the sugar by ¼ cup.

loaded applesauce muffins

Prep Time: 5 minutes | Cook Time: 20 minutes

Applesauce makes the best, most scrumptious muffins that don't dry out in a couple of days like other muffins do. Granted, *these* loaded applesauce muffins also take a bit of a trek through the garden with the addition of carrots, zucchini, and sunflower seeds. This recipe offers a great opportunity to incorporate some other sneaky ingredients while leaving the kids thinking that they're simply being spoiled with a sweet treat. The dried tart cherries do well at balancing out the sweetness of the carrots and the applesauce, so I think they are essential. But there is *definitely* room for personalization, so feel free to make it your own with the addition of other dried fruit and nuts. This culinary canvas is ready for you to decorate. Just don't let your toddler toss in glitter or dried macaroni. That I will *not* endorse.

Preheat the oven to 350°F. Grease two twelve-cup muffin tins or line them with paper liners.

In a large bowl, combine the flour, sugar, cinnamon, baking powder, baking soda, salt, ½ cup of the sunflower seeds, and the cherries.

In a small bowl, whisk together the vegetable oil, applesauce, and eggs.

Add the wet ingredients to the dry ingredients and stir to combine. Add the carrots and zucchini and stir until the batter is well mixed.

Scoop the batter into the prepared pans, filling the muffin cups three-quarters full. Top each muffin with 2 tablespoons of the sunflower seeds. Bake for about 20 minutes, until the tops spring back to the touch and a toothpick inserted into the center of a muffin comes out with just a couple of moist crumbs attached.

Serve warm, or let cool, then transfer to small zip-top bags and store in the fridge to pack in lunches for the rest of the week!

MAKES 24 MUFFINS

2½ cups all-purpose flour

1½ cups sugar

2 teaspoons ground cinnamon

2 teaspoons baking powder

1 teaspoon baking soda

1 teaspoon salt

1½ cups toasted unsalted hulled sunflower seeds

1½ cups dried tart cherries

1 cup vegetable oil

1 cup unsweetened applesauce

2 eggs

1 cup shredded carrots (about 4 medium)

1 cup shredded zucchini (about 2 small to medium)

Note

- These muffins sound sort of healthy, but they eat like super-moist carrot cake. If you're feeling indulgent, top them with cream cheese frosting and call them cupcakes!

triple coconut banana bread

Prep Time: 10 minutes | Cook Time: 60 to 70 minutes

MAKES ONE 9 X 5-INCH LOAF

Cooking spray or vegetable oil, for greasing

1 cup unsweetened shredded coconut

3 ripe medium bananas, plus 1 whole banana for garnish

½ cup coconut oil, melted

2 eggs

⅓ cup canned coconut milk

1 teaspoon vanilla extract

1¼ cups all-purpose flour

¾ cup whole wheat flour

2 tablespoons wheat germ

1½ cups sugar

1 teaspoon baking powder

1 teaspoon baking soda

½ teaspoon salt

Coconut is up there with butterscotch when it comes to my favorite ingredients. Believe it or not, coconut was *not* something that I liked early on in my career, but I'm pretty sure at some point, something significant happened in the structure of my DNA because I now crave coconut on the regular. (No, I'm not pregnant, but if I start dipping coconut in pickle juice, you have my permission to ask me that again.) This recipe incorporates the trifecta or "holy trinity" of coconut for any fellow fanatics: plain shredded coconut (in its simplest form), coconut milk, and coconut oil. These three things make this banana bread out-of-this-world! Sorry, guys—if you were looking for a cute family narrative to introduce this recipe, I have failed you. This one is all about *me* and my culinary faves!

Preheat the oven to 325°F. Grease a 9 x 5-inch loaf pan with pan spray or by brushing the sides and bottom with vegetable oil.

Spread the shredded coconut on a baking sheet and toast in the oven until golden brown, 5 to 6 minutes. Set aside to cool.

In a medium bowl, mash the 3 bananas with a fork until they are mostly smooth with a few small lumps (you should have 1½ cups mashed banana). Add the melted coconut oil, eggs, coconut milk, and vanilla and stir to combine.

In a separate bowl, whisk together the all-purpose flour, whole wheat flour, wheat germ, sugar, baking powder, baking soda, salt, and toasted coconut. Add the flour mixture to the banana mixture and stir until well combined. Pour the batter into the prepared loaf pan.

Peel the remaining banana and slice it in half lengthwise. Arrange the banana halves cut-side up on top of the batter in the pan and lightly press down so they are firmly adhered.

Bake the loaf for 60 to 70 minutes, until the top springs back to the touch and a toothpick inserted into the center of the loaf comes out clean with just a couple of moist crumbs clinging to it. When it is cool, wrap it tightly in plastic wrap and store on the counter for up to 5 days (if it lasts that long!). This banana bread is delicious served warm with a pat of salted butter, but the flavors really come alive after it has sat overnight at room temperature.

Notes

* Make sure you don't skip toasting the coconut—it adds an extra dimension of coconut flavor that you wouldn't get with raw coconut.

* This recipe isn't 100 percent healthy, but with whole wheat flour, wheat germ, and coconut oil, which add protein and fiber, you can feel slightly less guilty.

* Use ripe bananas for the best results, and serve a slice of this bread warm with salted butter for complete bliss.

pumpkin cream cheese streusel muffins

Prep Time: 10 minutes | Cook Time: 15 to 18 minutes

For years, pumpkin has been pigeonholed as a fall-only ingredient, but thanks to a growing acceptance for its year-round popularity, it is now enjoying liberation! This recipe incorporates all the things I loved most in baking school. Streusel (not just on top but *in* the muffin) and cream cheese are two ingredients that, whether together or apart, are surefire winners. (Maybe pause a moment and wipe the drool off your chin—you know your mouth is watering after reading that!) When we go to friends' houses and are asked to bring something, the self-induced pressure of being a professional chef kicks in, and I can't seem to let myself bring just a simple green salad (#PeoplePleaser). Instead, I bring these muffins. They are really easy to make and always prove to be a big hit. I warn you: You may be stuck making these for every single gathering in your foreseeable future. Please bake at your own risk!

Preheat the oven to 350°F. Line two twelve-cup muffin tins with paper liners or grease with cooking spray.

MAKE THE BATTER: In a large bowl, whisk together the flour, granulated sugar, brown sugar, cinnamon, ginger, salt, baking soda, cloves, and baking powder. In a separate bowl, stir together the eggs, pumpkin, vegetable oil, orange zest, and orange juice. Pour the wet ingredients into the dry ingredients and stir to combine. Set aside.

MAKE THE CREAM CHEESE FILLING: In a medium bowl with a handheld mixer, beat the cream cheese with the sugar until smooth. Add the lemon zest, lemon juice, vanilla, and egg and beat to combine. Set aside.

MAKES 24 MUFFINS

Cooking spray, for greasing (optional)

For the batter
3 cups all-purpose flour

1½ cups granulated sugar

1 cup brown sugar, lightly packed

1 tablespoon ground cinnamon

1 tablespoon ground ginger

2 teaspoons salt

2 teaspoons baking soda

1 teaspoon ground cloves

½ teaspoon baking powder

4 eggs

1 (15-ounce) can pure pumpkin puree

¾ cup vegetable oil

1 teaspoon grated orange zest

½ cup fresh orange juice

For the cream cheese filling
1 (8-ounce) package cream cheese, at room temperature

1 cup granulated sugar

½ teaspoon grated lemon zest

continued

pumpkin cream cheese streusel muffins, continued

1 tablespoon fresh lemon juice

½ teaspoon vanilla extract

1 egg

For the streusel

1 cup all-purpose flour

½ cup chopped pecans

½ cup brown sugar, lightly packed

2 tablespoons granulated sugar

¼ teaspoon salt

6 tablespoons (¾ stick) butter, melted

MAKE THE STREUSEL: In a medium bowl, whisk together the flour, pecans, brown sugar, granulated sugar, and salt. Add the melted butter and mix with a wooden spoon or your hands until the mixture looks like clumpy wet sand.

Fill the prepared muffin cups one-third full with batter. Add 1 tablespoon of the streusel to each muffin, then top with more batter to fill the cups three-quarters full. Transfer the cream cheese filling to a zip-top bag and snip off the corner. Pipe the filling into the center of the muffin batter, using 2 to 3 tablespoons per muffin. Cover the top of each muffin with a small handful of the streusel so the batter is not visible. The unbaked muffins should come just above the level of the muffin cups (don't worry—they will dome up as they bake and shouldn't spread to touch each other). Bake the muffins for 15 to 18 minutes, until the streusel is lightly browned and a toothpick inserted into the side of a muffin top comes out clean. Let them sit in the pans for 5 minutes, then gently remove them from the muffin tins and transfer to a wire rack to cool completely before storing in an airtight container or zip-top bag. They can be stored at room temp for 3 to 4 days or in the fridge for a week. Enjoy these warm from the oven or take them to your neighbors for a lovely holiday gift.

Notes

☆ Add semisweet chocolate chips to your batter for extra sweetness—pumpkin and chocolate go great together!

☆ You can bake this in a loaf pan instead. This recipe will make two small 6-inch loaves or one large 9-inch loaf, with a little batter leftover for a couple of muffins. Divide the batter between the pans and increase the baking time to 45 to 50 minutes.

any-day-ending-in-"y" overnight sticky buns

Prep Time: 45 minutes, plus 6+ hours for proofing overnight | Cook Time: 45 minutes

MAKES 12 STICKY BUNS

For the dough

1½ cups milk

2¼ teaspoons instant yeast (one ¼-ounce packet)

1 egg, at room temperature

8 tablespoons (1 stick) unsalted butter, melted

4 cups all-purpose flour

2 tablespoons granulated sugar

2 teaspoons baking powder

1½ teaspoons salt

For the filling

¾ cup packed brown sugar

4 tablespoons (½ stick) unsalted butter, at room temperature

2 teaspoons ground cinnamon

Like my deviled eggs (or a bad tattoo—did someone say "tribal armband"?), this is one of those recipes that has followed me *everywhere*. I am asked about my buns everywhere I go. I mean my *sticky* buns. Sheesh! I've been making this recipe since opening my first restaurant in the early 2000s. Now I make them for every single holiday and basically any day ending in "y." One of the biggest perks? You make these the night before! Refrigerate them overnight and then when you stumble into the kitchen at zero-dark-thirty for your dose of morning caffeine, bring them out, let the oven preheat, and before you know it these buns will be filling your house with the scent of caramel and cinnamon. Take these to a potluck, or make them for Christmas morning or just for a day of "Netflix and chill."

MAKE THE DOUGH: Combine ½ cup of water and milk in a glass measuring cup and microwave on high, or heat in a small saucepan over low heat for 1 minute, until just above lukewarm. The liquid should feel just slightly cooler than bathwater. Pour the liquid into the bowl of a stand mixer, add the yeast, egg, and melted butter, and whisk vigorously to combine. Add the flour, granulated sugar, baking powder, and salt. Mix by hand with a wooden spoon until the dough comes together and there are no dry spots. Put the bowl on the stand mixer fitted with the dough hook and knead on low speed for 5 minutes. The dough should be pretty sticky but not so wet that it doesn't come away from the sides of the bowl as it mixes. If it is a little too wet, add a tablespoon or two of flour. If it is so dry that the dough ball is slapping around the bowl, add a couple tablespoons of warm water. (If you don't have a mixer, you can knead the dough by hand on the countertop, but it will be pretty sticky, so be ready with some flour for dusting the counter and your hands.)

Transfer the dough to a large oiled bowl. Cover with plastic wrap and put the bowl in a warm spot to rise for 30 minutes.

continued

For the caramel

Cooking spray

2⅓ cups packed brown sugar

¼ cup light corn syrup

8 ounces (2 sticks) unsalted butter

¾ cup buttermilk

¼ cup heavy cream

½ teaspoon salt

MEANWHILE, MAKE THE FILLING: In a small bowl, stir together the brown sugar, butter, and cinnamon until smooth.

MAKE THE CARAMEL: Grease a 9 x 13-inch baking pan with cooking spray or butter.

When the dough has been rising for 20 minutes, in a large pot, combine the brown sugar, corn syrup, and butter and bring to a boil over medium-high heat, stirring continuously, then boil for 3 minutes without stirring.

While whisking continuously, extremely slowly and carefully add the buttermilk, cream, and salt and whisk until fully incorporated. Bring the caramel back to a boil and cook for 2 minutes more. Take the finished caramel off the heat and immediately pour it into the prepared pan. Set aside.

SHAPE THE BUNS: Transfer the dough to a lightly floured countertop. Press the dough out with your hands into a 14 x 10-inch rectangle about ½ inch thick. Spread the brown sugar filling over the entire surface of the dough, leaving 1 inch exposed along one long edge for sealing the roll.

Starting from the opposite long edge, tightly roll up the dough jelly-roll style until you get to the edge with no filling. Pinch the dough together to seal it up. Position the filled log seam-side down and slice it crosswise into 12 even(ish) pieces. (Use a sharp chef's knife or serrated cake knife to make sure you are cleanly slicing, not smashing, the log.)

Place the cinnamon rolls on top of the hot caramel in the pan, positioning them in 3 rows of 4 rolls each. Immediately cover the pan tightly with plastic wrap and refrigerate overnight or for up to 24 hours. (They should rest in the fridge for at least 6 hours but should not go longer than 24 hours or the yeast will become inactive.)

In the morning, preheat the oven to 350°F. Pull the pan from the fridge and set it on the counter to come to room temperature while the oven heats.

Uncover the rolls and bake until golden brown and cooked through, about 45 minutes. (You may want to put the pan on a baking sheet before putting it in the oven to catch any caramel that bubbles up during baking.) Let the sticky buns cool for at least 10 to 15 minutes before serving. (This is so important; if you turn them out too soon, you could seriously burn yourself, and the caramel will be so hot that it will run everywhere. They should still be very warm when you turn them over, though, so don't let them rest longer than 20 to 30 minutes.)

Cover the baking pan with an upside-down serving platter or an upside-down baking sheet lined with parchment paper. Very carefully flip the pan and the platter over, dumping the rolls onto the platter. The caramel should mostly stay on top of the rolls, but there will be a lot of caramel running off and onto the platter (good for scooping up!).

Notes

- If you want these to have nuts like a traditional sticky bun, add 2 cups chopped nuts (pecans, cashews, macadamias, your choice!) to the caramel in the baking dish before you add the cinnamon rolls. You could even add nuts to the filling.

- You can make these the same day. Just leave the covered sticky buns on the counter to rise instead of putting them in the fridge; they should double in size in 30 minutes to 1 hour. Then pop them straight into the oven.

- For extra indulgence, serve these warm buns with whipped cream on the side.

best sweet cornbread ever with honey butter

Prep Time: 5 minutes | Cook Time: 45 minutes

MAKES ONE 8-INCH SQUARE PAN

8 tablespoons (1 stick) unsalted butter, at room temperature

1 tablespoon plus 1 teaspoon honey

1¼ teaspoons salt

1½ cups all-purpose flour

1 cup fine cornmeal

1 cup sugar

1 tablespoon baking powder

2 large eggs

1⅓ cups whole milk

½ cup vegetable oil

Cornbread can be so much more than a side dish for chili. The first time I made this cornbread for my wife, she almost lost her *mind* about how awesome it was. Since that moment ten years ago, it has become a holiday favorite at our family gatherings. As for leftovers, I have a few preferred ways to enjoy this cornbread on days two, three, or four. Wait, who am I kidding? It never lasts past day two! I love taking a big piece, searing it in a hot pan with butter, and then serving it with a salad of bitter greens with buttermilk dressing. It is also really fun to use it in place of regular toast as a bed for poached eggs. Even though these two options are delectable, I'm a purist, so for me, nothing beats eating it straight out of the oven, with honey butter slathered on top. As a kid, I remember watching my dad eat his cornbread by dipping it in milk, and I was equally as puzzled as I was jealous that I had not thought of doing this myself! As an adult, I realized that I have formed my own goofy food-eating habits, and my theory has now become "whatever works for you!"

Preheat the oven to 325°F. Line the bottom and two sides of an 8-inch square baking pan with parchment paper, allowing 2 inches of overhang on each side.

In a small bowl by hand or with an electric mixer, whip together the butter, honey, and ¼ teaspoon of the salt until smooth. Set aside.

In a large bowl using a whisk, mix the flour, cornmeal, sugar, baking powder, and remaining 1 teaspoon salt until evenly combined. In another bowl, whisk together the eggs, milk, and vegetable oil until well combined. Pour the egg mixture into the flour mixture and mix thoroughly until combined and smooth. Transfer the batter to the prepared pan and smooth the top.

Bake the cornbread until a toothpick inserted into the center comes out with a few moist crumbs attached, 40 to 45 minutes. Let cool for 15 minutes before carefully lifting the cornbread out of the pan and peeling off the parchment. Cut the cornbread into squares and serve warm or at room temperature, slathered with the salted honey butter.

Notes

★ Wrap any cooled leftover cornbread tightly in plastic wrap and store at room temperature for up to 3 days.

★ Refrigerate the salted honey butter between uses.

★ This cornbread is southern-style sweet cornbread, so it's sweet like cake. If you want it slightly less sweet, reduce the sugar to ¾ cup.

★ You can make this recipe a little more savory by adding a can of drained roasted chilis (like Ro*Tel) or diced fresh jalapeño or bell pepper to the batter with the wet ingredients.

quick-change avocado toast

Prep Time: 10 minutes | Cook Time: 5 minutes

MAKES 4 SERVINGS

4 ripe medium to large avocados

1 tablespoon lemon juice

½ teaspoon garlic salt

Small pinch of red pepper flakes (optional)

3 dashes of Tabasco sauce (optional)

4 slices sourdough or multigrain bread

4 tablespoons (½ stick) unsalted butter, at room temperature

Additional toppings, as desired (see page 54)

Let me be completely honest: in some places, avocado toast is so overdone that it runs the risk of losing its "cool" factor. But please believe me, you cannot go wrong with this combination, and I will *never* get tired of it. When it comes to avocados, you literally have to pry them out of the hands of my wife and daughter. If fruit were a rock star and my girls were groupies, they would be following the avocado tour bus across the country and in the front row at every show. We are a family of three, but we eat five to ten avocados a week! I treat the process of making avocado toast like a Bloody Mary bar. I put the avocado mash on buttery, pan-toasted bread and from there people can add whatever toppings they desire from the "garnish bar." Nothing makes having company easier than when you have your guests assemble their own perfect meals!

Carefully cut the avocados in half around the pit and twist to open. Remove the pits (reserve 1 of the pits) and scoop the flesh out of the skins into a medium bowl. Add the lemon juice, garlic salt, red pepper flakes, and Tabasco (if using). Use a fork or whisk to chop up and mix the avocado until it is well mashed, with a few chunks remaining. Add the reserved pit and set aside while you toast the bread.

Spread 1 tablespoon of the butter on one side of each slice of bread. Place the bread buttered-side down in a large skillet and toast over medium heat until it is well browned and crisp on the bottom, 4 to 5 minutes. Flip the bread and toast until just lightly toasted on the second side, 1 to 2 minutes.

Spread one-quarter of the avocado mash on the buttered side of each slice of toast, smoothing it all the way to the edges (every bite deserves to be the best bite!). Let everyone top their toast according to their tastes.

continued

Ryan -Scallions, chilis
- Hot Sauce

-Eggs
LESLEY ·Kale
-Brie

Olive -Eggs - Bacon

Garnish Bar

Ryan's Toppings

1 tablespoon chopped fresh chiles (like jalapeño and serrano)

Lots of hot sauce

Fresh scallions

Lesley's Toppings

½ cup loosely packed finely shredded raw kale leaves

1 scrambled egg

Ripened soft cheese (like Brie)

Olive's Toppings

1 tablespoon chopped cooked bacon

½ hard-boiled egg, chopped

Notes

★ Make sure your avocados are ripe before you start. They should give just slightly when gently squeezed.

★ I like making pan-toasted bread for this instead of using the toaster. The griddled toast stays crispier under the moisture of the avocado mash, and I love the juxtaposition of the crisp buttery top with the softer, lightly toasted bottom.

★ I usually buy a mix of ripe and unripe avocados so they will last me a week or two. I ripen the unripe ones on my windowsill and then store them in the fridge to slow the ripening process. If you need to rush it, try putting your unripe avocados in a paper bag with an apple; the apple naturally gives off ethylene, which speeds up ripening in other fruits and veggies.

★ To give you a few extra hours of freshness, you can add one avocado pit to the avocado mash, then cover it with a paper towel that has been dampened with a little bit of lemon juice and wrung out.

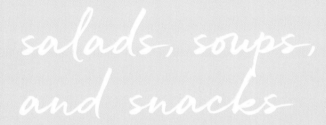

salads, soups, and snacks

apple, butternut squash, and quinoa salad

Prep Time: 5 minutes | Cook Time: 45 minutes

MAKES 4 SERVINGS

For the roasted squash

1 medium to large butternut squash, peeled, seeded, and cut into ½-inch cubes (about 6 cups)

3 tablespoons olive oil

½ teaspoon kosher salt

¼ teaspoon ground black pepper

For the dressing

½ cup vegetable oil

2 tablespoons white wine vinegar

1 tablespoon lemon juice

¾ teaspoon toasted sesame oil

1 tablespoon white miso paste

1 tablespoon Dijon mustard

1 tablespoon agave syrup

½ teaspoon sriracha

¼ teaspoon kosher salt

This is one of my most popular seasonal salads, both at my home and at my catering company, where I have been serving this for the last decade and a half. I love the versatility of this quinoa-based salad! It is a dish that lends itself well to changes in the ingredients to reflect the season: asparagus in spring, corn in the summer . . . you get the point. Instead of apples, try grapes, pears, or strawberries. This fun, light salad will be the perfect sidekick to a grilled chicken breast or roasted salmon. It can also stand alone as an incredible, healthy lunch. Using miso in this vinaigrette is *clutch*, and I promise that this dressing will become a staple in your house, so go out and stock up on some red or white miso (either will work just fine). Miso pairs really well in braises, especially those with pork or beef, so you'll get plenty of use out of it! A major heads-up, though: Miso is salty as heck, so a little goes a *long* way, but the umami that it provides is a big, giant YES.

ROAST THE SQUASH: Preheat the oven to 425°F. Line a baking sheet with aluminum foil or parchment paper.

Toss the squash, olive oil, salt, and pepper on the baking sheet to coat. Roast until tender when pierced with a fork and nicely browned in spots, 25 to 30 minutes.

MAKE THE DRESSING: In a blender, combine the vegetable oil, 2 tablespoons of water, vinegar, lemon juice, sesame oil, miso paste, mustard, agave, sriracha, and salt and blend until well combined. It's important to add the liquids before the miso to prevent the miso from getting stuck under the blades of the blender.

continued

For the salad

2 cups cooked quinoa (see the grain grid on page 176)

2 medium apples, cored and cut into wedges

4 cups baby greens, such as kale, baby spinach, arugula, or baby chard

ASSEMBLE THE SALAD: In a large bowl, combine the quinoa, roasted squash, and apples and toss with ⅓ cup of the dressing. It's okay if the squash or quinoa is still warm; they will absorb the dressing more that way and the salad will pack more punch. If you're serving the salad right away, add the baby greens and gently toss the salad, or store the greens, salad, and remaining dressing in separate airtight containers in the refrigerator for up to 3 days to eat later. You can use the remaining dressing to re-dress the salad if you find it has soaked up too much in the fridge. Be sure to keep the greens separate if you are storing the salad to serve later; they will wilt quickly once dressed.

Notes

- Make this a meal by topping the salad with grilled salmon, chicken, or steak.

- This salad is great to keep dressed and ready in the fridge for whenever you get hungry and need something healthy.

- The dressing makes more than you need for this amount of salad, and that's on purpose! I love keeping small jars of my homemade dressings in the fridge to use when I need to dress a quick green salad or veggies.

simplest marinated cherry tomato salad with 3/2/1 lemon-soy vinaigrette

Prep Time: 5 minutes, plus 1 to 4 hours for marinating | Cook Time: 0

In just a few minutes, you can have this salad on the table and fully dressed—even if you aren't! Just whip up the 3/2/1 vinaigrette ahead of time (it will become a new staple for your family, trust me) and get those tomatoes marinating! Soy and tomatoes are like Donny and Marie, Hoda and Jenna, or Cheech and Chong (for my San Francisco peeps). Honestly, the longer this salad sits, the better it gets, as the flavors continue to meld. A great trick and tip: Once you are down to the last bits of salad, throw some Dijon mustard in the bowl with all of the leftover juicy goodness. Mix the Dijon, the leftover salad, and the vinaigrette together and pulse it in the blender for a super-easy and delicious tomato-soy marinade for steak, pork chops, or whatever! This salad has now jumped into double duty. You'll have some extra dressing, so you can keep it in the fridge for other meals. It's my go-to basic vinaigrette for almost everything. I swear you could drizzle it over sheets of cardboard and I'd eat it. It's *that* crazy-good.

In a large, shallow dish or plastic container, combine the tomatoes and vinaigrette. (Make sure you use a large, shallow vessel for marinating so that all the tomatoes have contact with the vinaigrette.) Set aside at room temp for at least 1 hour or refrigerate for up to 4 hours.

Arrange a bed of arugula in a large salad bowl. Give the marinated tomatoes a final stir in the vinaigrette to coat them, then scoop them out onto the arugula. Sprinkle with the basil leaves and mozzarella (if using), and finish with a light sprinkling of Maldon salt and pepper before serving.

MAKES 4 SERVINGS

2 cups halved cherry tomatoes

1 cup 3/2/1 Lemon-Soy Vinaigrette (recipe follows)

1½ cups baby arugula

Leaves from 1 bunch basil, torn (about ½ cup)

1 cup fresh baby mozzarella balls (bocconcini or ciliegine, optional)

Maldon sea salt and freshly ground black pepper

Note

- **Get the kids involved by letting them shake the mason jar or whisk the vinaigrette in a bowl.**

continued

3/2/1 Lemon-Soy Vinaigrette

MAKES 2 CUPS

1 cup extra-virgin olive oil

⅔ cup fresh lemon juice (from 5 to 6 lemons)

⅓ cup liquid aminos or soy sauce

¼ teaspoon garlic salt

In a 1-quart mason jar or a plastic container with a tight-fitting lid, combine the olive oil, lemon juice, liquid aminos, and garlic salt. Cover and shake vigorously until emulsified. Store the vinaigrette in the fridge for up to 2 weeks.

don't-tell-anyone-it's-vegan swiss chard caesar salad with hand-torn croutons

Prep Time: 10 minutes | Cook Time: 15 minutes

MAKES 4 TO 6 SERVINGS

For the croutons

¼ cup olive oil

1 garlic clove, minced

½ teaspoon dried thyme

¼ teaspoon salt

¼ teaspoon ground black pepper

½ large loaf sourdough bread (unsliced)

For the dressing

½ cup silken tofu

3 tablespoons lemon juice

2 tablespoons olive oil

2 tablespoons capers

3 garlic cloves, peeled

2 teaspoons maple syrup

1 teaspoon Dijon mustard

1 teaspoon ground black pepper

½ teaspoon lemon zest

6 dashes of Tabasco sauce

My sister-in-law, Sherie, is not only a fabulous sister to my wife and an incredible auntie to Olive, but two years ago she also graciously stepped in as our full-time caregiver. We feel so honored and thankful to have her in that role. Along with all those things, she is also the "resident vegan" in our lives. I really can't thank her enough for being vegan, because it has made me think more about *what* and *how* I cook. It opened up a whole new door of food exploration for me and made me think more about preparing food with intention. She made me realize how much I was reaching for the cheese to finish off most of my dishes! Each Christmas, our families come together and I serve this "don't tell anyone it's vegan" salad alongside my mother-in-law's lasagna (check out page 103 for an adaptation of that dish), and nobody even *realizes* it's a vegan recipe. Even more shocking is that nobody even thinks to ask for the Parmesan! What I love about the dressing for this salad is that you can put it on romaine lettuce, shredded kale, Swiss chard, or whatever seasonal green your heart desires, making this is a year-round Caesar salad—grab what's in your garden and go with it. As a tip, reach for the silken tofu at the store. This will make the dressing extra creamy without having to use any eggs or mayonnaise. *Bon appétit!*

MAKE THE CROUTONS: Preheat the oven to 325°F. Line a baking sheet with parchment paper or aluminum foil.

In a large bowl, combine the olive oil, garlic, thyme, salt, and pepper. Tear the bread into bite-size chunks and add to the bowl. Toss the bread chunks in the oil mixture until they are well coated. Pour the bread onto the prepared baking sheet

continued

For the salad

3 bunches Swiss chard, leaves stemmed and chopped into bite-size pieces, or 1 large bag chopped chard leaves

and arrange the chunks in a single layer. Bake until they are toasted and golden brown, about 15 minutes. The edges will be dark brown, and there should still be just a touch of softness in the centers.

MAKE THE DRESSING: In a food processor or blender, combine the tofu, lemon juice, olive oil, capers, garlic, maple syrup, mustard, pepper, lemon zest, and Tabasco. Process the dressing until smooth.

ASSEMBLE THE SALAD: Place the chard in a large salad bowl and pour over half the dressing. Top with the croutons (it's okay if they are still slightly warm) and toss everything together to coat. If you prefer more dressing, add it to your taste. The dressing keeps well in the fridge, so any extra can be saved for later.

Note

★ Making croutons is a great way to use stale bread. Also, you don't have to use unsliced bread. If all you've got is sliced sourdough or French bread, just cut or tear it into hunks.

vegan orange–pine nut green bean salad

Prep Time: 5 minutes | Cook Time: 3 minutes | Inactive time: 15 minutes

As a kid, I thought green beans *only* came from a can. They were always a watery, suspicious-colored green mess. Maybe the fear of being forced to eat canned vegetables for every meal was the reason I didn't join the army. But nowadays stores usually have fresh, trimmed, cleaned green beans ready for you any day of the year. I use haricots verts, which are thin green beans, for this dish. You can make a crunchy vegetable salad seven days a week, no matter the season. I love the toasted, buttery, pine nuts in this recipe, but you can replace them with walnuts or cashews if you like. This totally vegan dressing has about half as much fat as other vinaigrettes because of the generous amount of orange juice it includes. Be sure to dress the green beans while they are hot so they soak up all the delicious sauce.

MAKE THE DRESSING: In a blender, combine the orange juice, lemon juice, vinegar, agave, mustard, olive oil, salt, pepper, Tabasco, and garlic. Blend until smooth, 1 to 2 minutes.

MAKE THE SALAD: Bring a large pot of water (4 to 6 quarts) to a boil and add 2 tablespoons of the salt. Add all the green beans at once and give them a stir. Boil for 3 minutes (set a timer). Turn off the heat and drain the green beans in a colander. Immediately transfer to a rimmed baking sheet and pour all the dressing over the top. Add the remaining 1 teaspoon salt and use tongs to stir the green beans and dressing. Once the beans have cooled enough to touch, use your hands to gently massage the dressing into the beans and press them into the dressing at the bottom of the pan. Let the green beans sit in the dressing until they are

MAKES 4 TO 6 SERVINGS

For the dressing

½ cup fresh orange juice (from 2 medium)

2 tablespoons lemon juice

1 tablespoon apple cider vinegar

2 teaspoons agave syrup

1½ teaspoons Dijon mustard

¼ cup olive oil

¾ teaspoon kosher salt

½ teaspoon ground black pepper

4 dashes of Tabasco sauce

1 garlic clove, peeled

For the salad

2 tablespoons plus 1 teaspoon kosher salt

1 (24-ounce) bag cleaned raw green beans

2 small bunches dill, coarsely chopped (about ½ cup packed)

1 cup raw pine nuts

continued

completely cool and have soaked up the dressing, 10 to 15 minutes. Add the dill and pine nuts, and give the salad another few turns in the pan to coat the ingredients with the dressing. Pour the salad into a serving bowl and drizzle the dressing left in the pan over the top.

Notes

⭐ When chopping fresh dill, remove as much of the tender "leaves" from the thick stem parts as you can, then just do a very coarse chop with a chef's knife. This recipe is really great with larger pieces of dill, as long as you remove any hardy stems.

⭐ This recipe is so quick and no-fuss because you don't have to shock the green beans in ice water after blanching. Instead, the cooking process is stopped by laying the green beans flat on a baking sheet and immediately dressing them. This technique also allows the green beans to soak up the dressing as they cool, making for a super-flavorful salad.

slow cooker creamy tomato soup with cheesy waffle dippers

Prep Time: 5 minutes | Cook Time: 3 to 4 hours

Move over Campbell's! There's a new tomato soup in town! I am probably gaining weight by just *talking* about this recipe, but don't run away in scale-tipping fear. This soup does contain heavy cream, but if you're going to indulge, do it right. The cream is absolutely essential, and takes this soup from good to *fabulous* faster than you can say "I'd like seconds." This is my revamp of an old childhood favorite, with waffle dippers replacing the classic grilled cheese. There is nothing better than dipping a crispy, Parmesan-basil waffle into a bowl of creamy tomato soup. Let the rainy days come. You'll be set.

Combine all the ingredients in a slow cooker and stir to combine. Cover the slow cooker and cook on high for 3 hours. (Alternatively, combine the ingredients in a large pot, cover, and cook over low heat, stirring occasionally, for 3 to 4 hours, until the onion and tomato pieces are soft and falling apart.)

Turn the heat off and let the soup cool for 15 to 20 minutes. Working in batches, transfer the soup to a blender and carefully puree until smooth. (The hot liquid will expand a little as it blends and could make a big dangerous mess, so don't fill the blender more than two-thirds full per batch.)

Serve the soup with the waffles alongside. Store leftover soup in an airtight container in the fridge for up to 1 week.

MAKES 6 SERVINGS

2 (28-ounce) cans whole or diced San Marzano tomatoes

2 cups heavy cream

1 onion, cut into large chunks

3 garlic cloves, peeled

½ bunch basil, leaves and stems included, plus more for garnish

1½ teaspoons salt

2 tablespoons agave syrup or honey

Cheesy Waffles (recipe follows), for serving

continued

Cheesy Waffles

Prep Time: 10 minutes | Cook Time: 15 minutes

MAKES 4 SERVINGS

2 cups all-purpose flour

½ cup cornmeal

2 teaspoons baking powder

1½ teaspoons salt

1 teaspoon sugar

½ teaspoon ground black pepper

½ teaspoon dried basil

¼ teaspoon onion powder

2 cups shredded Parmesan cheese

1 cup shredded mozzarella or provolone cheese

2 cups milk

2 eggs

8 tablespoons (1 stick) unsalted butter, melted

Cooking spray, for greasing

Preheat a waffle iron to medium-high heat.

In a medium bowl, whisk together the flour, cornmeal, baking powder, salt, sugar, pepper, basil, and onion powder until combined. Stir in ½ cup of the Parmesan and the mozzarella. In a separate bowl, whisk the milk and eggs together. Add the milk mixture to the dry ingredients and whisk just until the flour is moistened. Add the melted butter and mix just until the batter comes together. There should still be some lumps (just like pancake batter!).

Spray both plates of the waffle iron generously with cooking spray. Sprinkle 1 tablespoon of the Parmesan onto each quarter of the waffle iron, then immediately top with batter, using about ¼ cup per quarter. Close the waffle iron and cook for 6 to 8 minutes, until the steam from the waffle iron subsides and, if you take a little peek, the waffle is golden brown. Transfer the waffle to a wire rack and repeat to cook the rest of the batter. (If desired, you can keep the rack in the oven at 200°F to keep the waffles warm.)

Cut the waffles into sticks or wedges for easy dipping, and enjoy! Leftover waffles can be stored in a zip-top bag at room temperature for 2 to 3 days.

Notes

⭐ The waffles reheat nicely in the toaster.

⭐ This recipe makes a lot of soup, but that's how I roll; leftovers are my jam.

⭐ I always use San Marzano tomatoes for soup. I really think they have the best balance of acidity and sweetness.

super veggie chili con corny

Prep Time: 10 minutes | Cook Time: 3 hours

I find myself craving this dish in the cold of winter or on cool, foggy days (pretty much every summer day in the Bay Area). It is a reliable and always-delicious recipe when you're looking for a simple vegetarian meal. As a bonus, it freezes really well. Not only does the "corny" part of the title come from the corn in this veggie chili, but also from a childhood memory of going to the ballpark and pouring chili over a bag of corn chips. Some habits die hard and I can't imagine chili without this little ritual or a crunchy ingredient.

In a large pot or Dutch oven, heat the olive oil over high heat. Add the bell pepper, onions, mushrooms, garlic, and jalapeño and sauté until the onions become translucent, about 6 minutes. Add the tomato paste, salt, taco seasoning, and chili powder. Stir to combine and coat all the veggies with tomato paste. Cook over high heat, stirring frequently, until the spices become fragrant and the tomato paste darkens a little, 3 to 5 minutes. Add the diced tomatoes, corn, and black beans and stir to combine. Use a wooden spoon to scrape up any bits of browned tomato paste that may be stuck to the bottom of the pot. If using a slow cooker, transfer the chili to your slow cooker, cover, and cook on high for 3 hours. If cooking on the stovetop, reduce the heat to low, cover the pot, and cook, stirring occasionally, for 3 hours.

Turn off the heat and add the brown sugar and vinegar. Stir well to combine.

Serve the chili with all the fixings and be sure to save some for leftovers—the spices really bloom overnight and this dish tastes incredible the next day.

Note

⭐ If you're using an Instant Pot, use the Sauté function to sauté the veggies, tomato paste, and spices before adding the tomatoes, corn, and beans. Then switch to Slow Cook, cover, and cook on medium for 3 hours.

MAKES 4 TO 6 SERVINGS

2 tablespoons olive oil

2 cups diced bell peppers (2 small to medium)

2 cups diced onions (2 small to medium)

2 cups diced mushrooms (6 ounces)

3 garlic cloves, minced (about 1 tablespoon)

½ large jalapeño, minced

1 (6-ounce) can tomato paste

2 teaspoons salt

2 tablespoons taco seasoning (page 135 or store-bought)

1½ tablespoons chili powder

1 (28-ounce) can diced San Marzano tomatoes

1 (16-ounce) bag frozen corn

1 (15-ounce) can black beans, drained

1 tablespoon brown sugar

1 tablespoon apple cider vinegar

Garnishes

Sour cream

Queso fresco

Chopped scallions

Pickled jalapeños

Fresh cilantro leaves, whole or chopped

Corn chips or tortilla chips

must-try peanut butter–glazed chicken wings with ginger-scallion relish

Prep Time: 40 minutes | Cook Time: 40 minutes

MAKES 4 SERVINGS

For the marinated chicken

1 garlic clove, minced

2 tablespoons rice vinegar

2 tablespoons olive oil

1 teaspoon salt

¼ teaspoon ground black pepper

2 to 3 pounds chicken wings, drumettes separated from flats

For the peanut butter glaze

¼ cup coconut milk

¼ cup creamy peanut butter

2 tablespoons lemon juice

2 tablespoons honey

1 tablespoon low-sodium soy sauce

½ teaspoon sriracha

½ teaspoon sesame oil

¼ teaspoon fish sauce

¼ teaspoon ground ginger

Attention, all skeptical home chefs! Don't let this recipe name scare you. Traditional Vietnamese and Thai restaurants incorporate incredible peanut sauces in their dishes, and they are to *die* for. This is my version of a chicken satay. Except mine is without the actual "satay" (skewers cooked on the grill) . . . and I use drumettes, so really, I guess it's not even close. But please hang with me. This is a great dish to bring to a party or a Super Bowl gathering. It's a perfect quick snack and finger food. As the title says, there's peanut butter in the glaze, so those with peanut allergies, take note. The ginger-scallion relish on the side is absolutely essential. This is a deceivingly delicious dish. I mean, peanut butter and *jelly* has been a winning combo since before we can remember, so let's push this peanut butter and *chicken* recipe to the forefront so it can gain some fame as well!

MARINATE THE CHICKEN: In a gallon-size zip-top bag, combine the garlic, rice vinegar, olive oil, salt, and pepper. Add the chicken and seal the bag. Massage the bag, mixing all the marinade ingredients and working the marinade into the wings. Set the bag of wings aside to marinate for at least 30 minutes and up to 4 hours.

MAKE THE GLAZE: If the coconut milk is chunky, heat it in the microwave to melt the fat solids before using it. In a medium bowl, whisk together the peanut butter, coconut milk, lemon juice, honey, 2 tablespoons of water, soy sauce, sriracha, sesame oil, fish sauce, and ginger until well combined. Set aside.

continued

must-try peanut butter–glazed chicken wings with ginger-scallion relish, continued

For the scallion-ginger relish

1 small bunch scallions, thinly sliced (¾ cup), plus more for garnish

1 tablespoon lemon juice

2 teaspoons minced fresh ginger

1 teaspoon rice vinegar

1 teaspoon sesame oil

¼ teaspoon ground black pepper

¼ teaspoon salt

¼ cup olive oil

2 tablespoons baking powder

½ cup crushed roasted salted peanuts, for garnish

MAKE THE RELISH: In a small bowl, combine the scallions, lemon juice, ginger, vinegar, sesame oil, pepper, salt, and olive oil. Set aside.

COOK THE WINGS: Preheat the oven to 450°F. Line a baking sheet with parchment paper or aluminum foil.

Spread the wings in a single layer on a few paper towels laid out on the counter. Use another couple of paper towels to blot the moisture from the tops of the wings, and give each wing a little squeeze with the towels. The point is to remove as much moisture as possible, helping to create a really crispy skin on the wings when they bake.

Transfer the wings to a large bowl, add the baking powder, and toss, being sure to coat the wings evenly. Lay the wings in a single layer on the prepared baking sheet. Bake for 25 minutes. Carefully remove the baking sheet from the oven and flip each wing over. Return them to the oven and bake until nicely browned and crispy, about 15 minutes.

Toss the hot crispy wings in the glaze to coat, then transfer them to a serving dish. Drizzle the scallion-ginger relish over the wings and garnish with the peanuts.

Note

* If the wings are still intact when you buy them, don't worry, it's easy to break them down. Bend the joint backward and use a sharp knife to separate the drumette from the flat. Then cut the wing tip from the flat in the same way. (Discard the tip or use it for chicken stock.)

triple-napkin pull-apart hot sub bake

Prep Time: 10 minutes | Cook Time: 15 minutes

Living in San Francisco for twenty-two years, I have experienced a *lot* of amazing charcuterie. It inspired me to create this super-simple sub-sandwich appetizer. My wife and my dad, Danny, could live on charcuterie alone. When they are together, there is always an abundance of salami, mortadella, and fabulous cheeses on the counter. (The board is also wiped clean pretty quickly!) Here I've combined them with our family's favorite King's Hawaiian rolls—an incredible mash-up. It really could not be simpler. You use an entire package of these rolls, stuff them, dress them, and bake them until hot and melty. Then just let people dig in! This is my game-day favorite. If you ever need a dish for an office cooking competition, trust me, you'll want to make this. The serving size is, of course, only a suggestion. If you don't pull it apart, it's technically only one serving, right?

Preheat the oven to 400°F.

Chop the olives and pepperoncini by hand or in a food processor until chunky. Add the red pepper flakes, Italian seasoning, and olive oil and set aside.

Melt the butter in the microwave or in a small saucepan over low heat. Add ¼ cup of the dressing and stir to combine. If the mixture firms up too much to brush easily, microwave it for another 10 seconds or return to the stove over low heat to warm it up.

Split the rolls in half horizontally and lay the bottom halves in an 8-inch square baking dish. Set the top buns on a separate baking sheet and brush them on both sides with half the dressing-butter mixture. Set the baking sheet aside.

Brush the remaining dressing-butter mixture over the bottom buns. Arrange all the meats on the buns and top with the provolone.

MAKES 6 SERVINGS

½ cup pitted Kalamata olives

¼ cup jarred pepperoncini

Pinch of red pepper flakes

1 teaspoon Italian seasoning

1 tablespoon olive oil

4 tablespoons (½ stick) unsalted butter

¼ cup plus 2 tablespoons red wine dressing (try the dressing from my Slam Dunk Salami Rolls, page 82)

12 King's Hawaiian original sweet rolls

6 ounces sliced spicy capicola

6 ounces sliced dry salami

6 ounces sliced prosciutto

8 slices provolone cheese

6 ounces fresh mozzarella cheese

½ head iceberg lettuce, very thinly sliced (like angel hair slaw)

12 large basil leaves, thinly sliced

1 medium tomato, thinly sliced

continued

triple-napkin pull-apart hot sub bake, continued

Spread the olive-pepperoncini mixture on top of the provolone, then cover it with the fresh mozzarella. Put the baking dish on the top shelf in the oven and the baking sheet on the bottom shelf and bake until the cheese has all melted and the top buns are nicely toasted, about 15 minutes.

While the sandwiches are toasting, in a small bowl, toss the lettuce and basil with the remaining 2 tablespoons dressing.

To finish assembling the sandwiches, top the melted cheese with tomato slices and the dressed iceberg. Put the toasted bun tops on top of the iceberg slaw and secure with frilly toothpicks. Serve while warm and gooey.

Note

★ Feel free to omit the olives and/or pepperoncini if the kiddos don't like them. The gooey mozzarella and red wine dressing butter make this sandwich so good, even without the spice.

slam dunk salami rolls

Prep Time: 10 to 15 minutes | Cook Time: 0

MAKES 15 ROLLS

1 cup whipped cream cheese, at room temperature

¼ cup sun-dried tomato slices packed in oil, drained

15 slices pepper salami (the slices should be 3 to 4 inches across)

4 or 5 mild jarred pepperoncini, sliced

15 small to medium basil leaves

15 fresh baby mozzarella balls (bocconcini or ciliegine; optional)

¾ cup Red Wine Dressing (recipe follows)

Our friends Kristin and Jaren often bring their version of these irresistible appetizers to our house when we get together. I remember tasting them and saying, "Wait, they're just salami, cream cheese, and pepperoncini?" Sometimes simplicity is best, and sometimes I'm totally inspired by the culinary ventures of my friends! (Sometimes I also steal their recipes . . . #SorryNotSorry.) I've jazzed them up a little and added my favorite tangy Italian vinaigrette. Add these to your repertoire of bring-to-a-party favorites. I dare you to eat just one.

In a food processor, pulse the cream cheese and sun-dried tomatoes until smooth.

Lay the salami slices out flat on a cutting board. Put 1 teaspoon of the sun-dried tomato cream cheese in the center of each salami slice. Top the cream cheese with a slice or two of pepperoncini and a basil leaf. Roll the salami slice up, add a mozzarella ball if you like, and secure with a toothpick. Place the salami rolls on a serving platter.

Spoon the dressing over the rolls and serve.

Note

⭐ **This recipe is a great project for kids, and you can customize the ingredients for everyone's individual tastes.**

Red Wine Dressing

MAKES 1½ CUPS

1 cup extra-virgin olive oil

⅓ cup red wine vinegar

1 tablespoon lemon juice

1½ teaspoons dried oregano

1½ teaspoons dried basil

1 teaspoon garlic salt

1 teaspoon onion powder

Pinch of red pepper flakes

Combine all the ingredients in a mason jar. Close the lid and shake until well mixed. Store the dressing in the fridge for up to 2 weeks.

sweet-and-salty party mix

Prep Time: 5 minutes | Cook Time: 35 minutes

MAKES 1 FULL GALLON ZIP-TOP BAG

1 egg white

¼ cup granulated sugar

¼ cup brown sugar, lightly packed

¾ teaspoon chili powder

1¾ teaspoons salt

1½ cups raw whole almonds

1½ cups raw whole cashews

8 tablespoons (1 stick) unsalted butter

1½ tablespoons Worcestershire sauce

¾ teaspoon Old Bay seasoning

½ teaspoon garlic salt

½ teaspoon onion powder

½ teaspoon dried thyme

2 cups unsweetened bran cereal

2 cups wheat squares cereal

1½ cups rice squares cereal

1½ cups pretzel sticks

1 cup honey O's cereal

1 cup dried blueberries

1 cup dried cherries or cranberries

This is less of a recipe and more "instructions for assembly." You might know this popular style of party mix as "nuts and bolts"—my brother-in-law, Justin, makes *his* version for the holidays (Justin, I told you I would mention you in the cookbook!). I've put my own spin on it, and renamed it to match. This is a great snack during the holidays, or if you're scared by the ingredient list on the back of store-bought party mixes where the sugar and salt content is always through the roof, not to mention the unpronounceable ingredients! This mix is a perfect addition to a cheese plate, a great snack to set out for yourself or guests while watching a game, an ideal treat to sneak into the movies, and a fun on-the-go nosh. It is also a tasty and easy munchie for kids, and kids are *always* hungry! Olive eats it by the handful, and so do I.

Preheat the oven to 300°F. Line a baking sheet with parchment paper or aluminum foil.

In a large bowl, combine the egg white, granulated sugar, brown sugar, chili powder, and ¾ teaspoon of the salt. Add the almonds and cashews and toss until the nuts are coated with the egg white mixture. Use your hands to rub the sugared egg whites into the nuts to make sure they are fully coated. Pour the nuts onto the prepared baking sheet and arrange them in a single layer. Bake the nuts until they are medium-brown in color and the sugars have crystallized, about 15 minutes.

In a small saucepan, melt the butter over low heat, then cook over low heat until the solids at the bottom of the pan start to turn brown. Turn the heat off and add the Worcestershire, Old Bay, garlic salt, onion powder, thyme, and remaining 1 teaspoon salt. Whisk to combine.

In a large bowl, combine all the cereals and pretzels. Pour the spiced butter mixture over the cereal and gently mix until all the pieces are well coated. Try not to break up the cereal too much. Spread the mixture over a baking sheet and bake until golden brown and fragrant, 20 to 25 minutes.

Let the cereal mixture and candied nuts cool completely. In a large bowl, gently combine the cereal mixture, nuts, blueberries, and cherries. Serve, or store the mix in an airtight container or gallon-size zip-top bag at room temperature for up to 2 weeks.

Note

★ The addition of the dried fruit really makes this mix stand out. I love the combination of sweet, savory, spicy, and salty.

pasta

date-night garlic shrimp rigatoni pasta

Prep Time: 15 minutes | Cook Time: 20 minutes

MAKES 6 SERVINGS

1 pound peeled and deveined large shrimp, halved from head to tail

4 tablespoons olive oil

10 garlic cloves: 5 minced, 5 smashed and peeled

½ teaspoon kosher salt, plus more as needed

Generous pinch of freshly ground black pepper

Generous pinch of cayenne pepper

16 ounces dried rigatoni

1 jalapeño, seeded and finely chopped

2 teaspoons all-purpose flour

½ cup dry vermouth

½ cup coarsely chopped fresh parsley leaves, plus more for serving

¾ cup clam juice

4 tablespoons (½ stick) unsalted butter, cubed

Zest and juice of 1 lemon

Shrimp is one of those proteins that everyone thinks they know how to cook, but believe me, it is easy to get it wrong. Please don't panic. I promise, you're already halfway there, and this recipe eliminates the questions and struggles of preparing shrimp properly. Shrimp can be a temperamental little sea creature, and it will need all two minutes of your undivided attention (#GetOffInstagramWhileCookingShrimp). This recipe allows you to have a successful and romantic (wink-wink) date-night kind of night, with a fabulous meal as the centerpiece. I vividly recall trying to flex my culinary muscle the first year that my wife and I were dating. I prepared what seemed like every sea-going creature just to impress her. Shrimp are easy to find at any grocery store (I prefer larger shrimp that are deveined and peeled for ease), and this recipe is great when you are in a pinch and need a fabulous (but stress-free) meal.

In a medium bowl, combine the shrimp, 2 tablespoons of the olive oil, 1 tablespoon of the minced garlic, the salt, black pepper, and cayenne. Mix well to coat the shrimp and set aside.

In a large stockpot, bring 6 quarts generously salted water to a rolling boil. Add the rigatoni and cook until 1 minute short of al dente. Reserve 1 cup of the pasta water and drain the pasta.

Meanwhile, in a large high-sided skillet, combine the remaining 2 tablespoons olive oil and the 5 smashed garlic cloves. Cook over medium heat, stirring, until the garlic is golden brown, about 4 minutes. Use a slotted spoon to remove the garlic and discard it. Add the marinated shrimp to the pan, along with any juices that have accumulated in the bowl. Spread the shrimp in an even layer and cook, undisturbed, for 2 minutes. Transfer the shrimp to a plate.

continued

date-night garlic shrimp rigatoni pasta, continued

Add the remaining minced garlic and the jalapeño to the skillet and cook until fragrant, about 1 minute. Sprinkle in the flour and cook, stirring continuously, for 1 minute. Add the vermouth and cook, stirring continuously, to cook off the alcohol, about 1 minute. Add the parsley and clam juice and stir to combine. Increase the heat to high and bring to a boil. Cook, stirring continuously, until the sauce reduces and thickens, 2 to 3 minutes. Remove the skillet from the heat and add the butter, lemon zest, and lemon juice. Stir continuously until the butter has melted.

Return the skillet to the stovetop over medium heat. Add the pasta, shrimp, and ½ cup of the reserved pasta water (see Notes). Cook, stirring, until all the ingredients are fully combined and evenly coated with the sauce, about 1 minute. Sprinkle with parsley and serve.

Notes

★ **HALF COOKED?!** Don't worry! The shrimp will finish cooking in the sauce. Use this trick to keep shrimp from overcooking and becoming rubbery.

★ **Use extra pasta water to help resuscitate a sauce that has been sitting awhile. Seconds, anyone?**

★ **Leave in some of the jalapeño seeds for an extra kick!**

chicken caesar angel hair pasta

Prep Time: 15 minutes | Cook Time: 30 minutes

I have a culinary confession: I love store-bought salad dressing (and Sour Patch Kids, but believe me, they don't go well together). There are so many things that I love about chicken Caesar salad, so translating that into a pasta dish just made sense to me. The dressing in this recipe is a creamy store-bought version, and I've amped it up with bacon and Manchego cheese. Then there are the croutons (yes, croutons in pasta!). They are just *amazing,* and always seem to be the first suspect to leave the scene by way of immediate consumption!

In a large bowl, whisk together 1 tablespoon of the garlic, the salt, onion powder, garlic powder, and pepper. Add the chicken and toss to coat.

In a large skillet, heat the olive oil over medium-high heat. Add the chicken and cook, stirring, until browned, about 8 minutes. Using a slotted spoon, transfer the chicken to a plate.

In the same skillet, cook the bacon, stirring, until browned and crispy, about 5 minutes. Using a slotted spoon, transfer the bacon to a paper towel–lined dish. Add the onion to the skillet and cook until translucent around the edges, about 3 minutes. Stir in the remaining 1½ teaspoons garlic and the thyme and cook for 2 minutes more. Stir in the broth, making sure to scrape up any browned bits on the bottom of the pan. Add the cream and cook until reduced by half, about 3 minutes. Stir in the Caesar dressing, return the chicken and any accumulated juices to the pan, and bring to a simmer. Remove from the heat. Stir in the lemon juice, parsley, and two-thirds of the bacon.

Meanwhile, in a large stockpot, bring 6 quarts generously salted water to a rolling boil. Add the pasta and cook 1 minute short of al dente. Reserve 1 cup of the pasta water and strain.

MAKES 6 SERVINGS

6 garlic cloves, minced (about 1½ tablespoons)

1 teaspoon salt, plus more as needed

½ teaspoon onion powder

½ teaspoon garlic powder

½ teaspoon ground black pepper

1 pound boneless, skinless chicken breasts, cut into 1-inch cubes

¼ cup extra-virgin olive oil

10 slices thick-cut bacon, chopped

1 small yellow onion, diced (1 cup)

2 tablespoons fresh thyme leaves

½ cup chicken broth

¼ cup heavy cream

1 (16-ounce) bottle creamy Caesar dressing

1 tablespoon lemon juice

¼ cup chopped fresh parsley, plus more for serving

16 ounces dried angel hair pasta

½ cup finely grated Parmesan cheese, plus more for serving

½ cup shaved Manchego cheese

continued

chicken caesar angel hair pasta, continued

Add the pasta, Parmesan, Manchego, and half the reserved pasta water to the sauce. Cook over medium heat until the sauce is silky, adding additional pasta water as needed, 1 to 2 minutes.

Plate the pasta in shallow bowls and sprinkle with the remaining bacon. Garnish with parsley, Parmesan, and the croutons and serve hot.

1 (5-ounce) package garlic croutons, lightly crushed, or 1 recipe croutons (page 64)

Note

★ When cooking angel hair pasta, I always pull it from the water just before it is cooked to al dente. That way, the super-thin pasta won't overcook when I combine it with the hot pasta sauce.

california-style puttanesca pasta

Prep Time: 10 minutes | Cook Time: 20 minutes

MAKES 2 TO 4 SERVINGS

4 cups dry red wine

1 tablespoon salt

8 ounces dried spaghetti

2 tablespoons olive oil

½ red onion, thinly sliced

4 anchovy fillets

5 garlic cloves, sliced into thin slivers

¼ cup pitted Kalamata olives, crushed or coarsely chopped

1½ tablespoons capers

1 pint cherry tomatoes

2 tablespoons unsalted butter

2 tablespoons good extra-virgin olive oil

1 bunch flat-leaf parsley, coarsely chopped (about 1 cup)

Freshly cracked black pepper

My father-in-law, Michael, is one of my best friends (and a good drinking buddy as well). He's an anchovy and sardine lover and he does not mind eating them straight out of the can. He often comes to stay with us or to help us watch Olive and, while I enjoy making foods that he loves, when I'm hosting people I don't always have a lot of time to prepare super-involved dishes. Luckily, I can make this recipe in a hurry by using one of Michael's favorite ingredients: anchovies. *Puttanesca* translates to . . . let's just say a not-very-family-friendly-cookbook kind of word, and definitely not a word that I want to use in a paragraph about my father-in-law. (If you're curious, look it up.) If you want a quick, saucy, tomato-y, herby pasta that is a bit salty and garlicky, take a stab at this recipe. (Although since the pasta is cooked in red wine, it's definitely a "grown-up" dish.) Add more anchovies, if you'd like, or remove some, but either way, this dish will be *banging* good. (Maybe that's the wrong choice of adjective to use when referring to a puttanesca pasta. Again, look it up!)

In a medium pot, bring the wine, 2 cups of water, and salt to a boil. Add the spaghetti and boil, stirring occasionally, for about 13 minutes.

While the spaghetti cooks, in a large sauté pan, heat the olive oil over medium heat. Add the onion, anchovies, and garlic. Use a wooden spoon to mash the anchovies into the onion and garlic, helping them to "melt." Sauté, stirring frequently, until the onion has softened and is almost translucent, about 4 minutes. Add the olives, capers, and tomatoes and stir to coat the tomatoes in oil. Raise the heat to medium-high and cook, undisturbed, until the tomatoes start to blister and pop, 4 to 5 minutes.

When the pasta is done cooking, drain it, reserving the cooking liquid. Turn the heat off and add the pasta to the sauté pan. Add ¼ cup of the cooking liquid, the butter, and the extra-virgin olive oil and toss to combine and coat the noodles. Once the butter has melted and all the ingredients are tossed together, add the parsley and give it one final toss. Transfer the finished pasta to a serving bowl and top with cracked black pepper.

Note

★ Don't add any additional salt! The brininess of the olives, capers, and anchovies is enough to season the whole dish—trust me.

three-cheese mac and cheese muffins

Prep Time: 15 minutes | Cook Time: 35 minutes

These cheesy little muffins are great for keeping in the freezer and then reheating for last-minute guests, or as a quick on-the-go snack for kids who never seem to sit still. They were loosely inspired by one of my signature dishes, the Mac and Cheese Spring Rolls from my book *One to Five* (a shameless plug, I know). Since that recipe is so darn popular, I reinvented it in a muffin tin version, an idea that came to me one day as I was staring at my muffin tins and talking to them (my quirky but usually effective way of willing new ideas to enter my brain). If you're in the mood for a healthier and maybe more traditional mac 'n' cheese option, check out my Cheesy Broccoli-Cheddar Bow Ties recipe on page 99.

MAKE THE CRUMB TOPPING: In a small bowl, stir together the butter, salt, panko, and Parmesan until well combined.

MAKE THE MAC AND CHEESE: Preheat the oven to 350°F. Spray 36 wells of two mini-muffin tins with cooking spray.

In a medium bowl, whisk together the sour cream, mustard, egg, and hot sauce.

In a large bowl, combine 2 cups of the cheddar, 1 cup of the Monterey Jack, and the flour and toss until well coated.

In a large skillet, melt the butter over medium-high heat. Add the half-and-half and bring to a simmer. Add the cheese-flour mixture and cook over medium heat, stirring continuously, until the cheese has melted, about 5 minutes.

Meanwhile, in a large stockpot, bring 6 quarts generously salted water to a rolling boil. Add the pasta and cook until 2 minutes short of al dente, then drain. Return the pasta to the stockpot, add the cheese sauce and the sour cream mixture, and stir well to combine.

MAKES 18 MUFFINS

For the crumb topping
4 tablespoons (½ stick) unsalted butter, melted

1 teaspoon kosher salt

1 cup panko bread crumbs

2 tablespoons grated Parmesan cheese

For the mac and cheese
Cooking spray, for greasing

½ cup sour cream

1 teaspoon Dijon mustard

1 large egg

3 or 4 dashes of hot sauce

3 cups shredded sharp cheddar cheese (8 ounces)

2 cups shredded Monterey Jack cheese (8 ounces)

¼ cup all-purpose flour

2 tablespoons unsalted butter

2 cups half-and-half

Salt

16 ounces dried elbow pasta

continued

three-cheese mac and cheese muffins, continued

Divide half the crumb topping among the wells of the prepared muffin tins and scoop heaping 2 tablespoon portions of the pasta on top of the crumbs. Using a teaspoon, make a small well in the center of the pasta mixture in each muffin cup. Sprinkle with the remaining cheese and top with the remaining crumb topping. Bake until golden brown, about 12 minutes. Let cool for 10 to 15 minutes before carefully removing the muffins from the pans with an offset spatula. Serve warm, or let cool completely, then store in an airtight container in the refrigerator for up to 5 days or freeze (see Note).

Note

★ To freeze leftover muffins, place them on a baking sheet and freeze until solid, then transfer to zip-top freezer bags and freeze for up to 2 months. To thaw and reheat, wrap each muffin in a slightly dampened paper towel and microwave for 45 to 60 seconds. Place thawed muffins into a buttered muffin tin and bake at 375°F until heated through, 12 to 15 minutes.

cheesy broccoli-cheddar bow ties

Prep Time: 5 minutes | Cook Time: 20 minutes

We all find ourselves facing the obligatory clean-out-the-fridge task every few weeks. If you're like me, you're probably left with a pile of random ingredients. I seem to be a repeat offender when it comes to buying too much spinach, kale, and arugula. Yes, my name is Ryan Scott, and I am a hoarder of greens. Phew. I feel better now. One night, back when Olive was in the midst of her terrible twos (and refusing to eat the greens that she couldn't get enough of just the week before), I was making mac and cheese and this recipe idea jumped into my brain. It's a bit reminiscent of a loaded baked potato with cheddar and broccoli, and the sauce uses up that extra spinach you might have left in the fridge. It's so versatile, too—you could puree butternut squash, zucchini, or carrots into the sauce as well, a great way to sneak in vegetables in a really tasty way.

In a large stockpot, bring 4 to 6 quarts generously salted water to a boil. Add the pasta and cook until al dente, 11 to 12 minutes. When the pasta is done, add the broccoli and turn the heat off. Let the broccoli float over the pasta for 1 minute—do not stir! After 1 minute, scoop the broccoli out of the pasta water with a slotted spoon and transfer it to a food processor. Drain the pasta and return it to the pot.

Add the spinach to the food processor and pulse until the vegetables are finely minced.

While the pasta cooks, melt the butter in a medium saucepan over medium heat. Stir in the flour and cook for 1 minute, whisking continuously. While whisking, add the milk. Bring the mixture to a simmer. Simmer the sauce for 1 minute, then turn the heat off and add the cheeses. Stir until the cheese has completely melted. Add the salt, mustard, and Tabasco; stir to combine. Stir in the broccoli-spinach mixture.

MAKES 6 TO 8 SERVINGS

2 teaspoons kosher salt, plus more as needed

16 ounces dried bow-tie (farfalle) pasta

1½ cups frozen broccoli

1 cup firmly packed baby spinach

4 tablespoons (½ stick) unsalted butter

¼ cup all-purpose flour

3½ cups milk

8 slices American cheese

2¼ cups shredded sharp cheddar cheese (8 ounces)

½ teaspoon Dijon mustard

4 dashes of Tabasco sauce

continued

cheesy broccoli-cheddar bow ties, continued

Pour the broccoli-cheese sauce over the hot pasta and fold until all the pasta is coated. It may look very saucy or loose, and that's okay. This recipe is big for a reason: I put most of it in portioned containers in the fridge for the family to eat all week; since it's so saucy we don't need to add any additional milk to reheat it. Store leftovers in airtight containers in the fridge for up to 6 days.

Note

⭐ **To make a hearty meal out of this, add shredded roasted chicken or diced ham, maybe even bacon and bread crumbs. This is a super-versatile, kid-friendly stovetop mac that can be tailored to anyone's tastes.**

mother-in-law-sagna cups

Prep Time: 20 minutes | Cook Time: 30 minutes

My mother-in-law, Bonnie, always hosts our big family Christmas at her house. For years, she would prepare for *three weeks* for the special meal. She took it very seriously and she always did an incredible job. One year, my wife suggested that we take the pressure off her mom by simplifying the big dinner, so for the last three years, Bonnie and I have done most of the cooking together on Christmas Eve. In the spirit of keeping things simple, we make her signature lasagna and my Swiss chard Caesar salad (page 64), and that's it! The meat eaters are happy, the two vegans in the family are happy, and . . . to all a good night! Truth be told, I crave her lasagna more than once a year, so I created a simpler, faster version using wonton wrappers instead of lasagna noodles. I also bake this recipe in a muffin tin instead of a huge Pyrex dish, so that everyone gets a perfectly portioned serving. They bake in just over half an hour and also freeze really well. Here's the fun part: gather your ingredients—your wonton wrappers, sautéed meat, ricotta cheese mix, and jarred sauce. Now you and the kids are all set to build these little cups. Thank you, Bonnie!

Preheat the oven to 325°F. Liberally spray 16 wells of two twelve-cup muffin tins with cooking spray.

Combine the olive oil, grated onion (with any juice released while grating), and garlic in a large saucepan or Dutch oven, turn the heat to medium-high, and cook until the onion softens and the garlic becomes fragrant, about 5 minutes. Add the ground beef and sausage and stir to break up the meat and mix with the onion and garlic. Add the dried onion, 2 teaspoons of the garlic salt, 1 teaspoon of the black pepper, the garlic powder, dried basil, dried parsley, and red pepper flakes. Stir to combine, reduce the heat to medium, and cook until almost all the moisture has evaporated from the mixture, 12 to 15 minutes.

MAKES 16 LASAGNA CUPS

Cooking spray

2 tablespoons olive oil

1 medium yellow onion, grated (plus all of its juices)

2 tablespoons minced garlic

1 pound ground beef (90% lean)

1 pound loose mild Italian sausage

1 tablespoon dried onion

3 teaspoons garlic salt

1¼ teaspoons ground black pepper

1 teaspoon garlic powder

1 teaspoon dried basil

1 teaspoon dried parsley

⅛ teaspoon red pepper flakes

1 (25-ounce) jar marinara sauce (I like Trader Joe's Arrabiata)

2 cups full-fat ricotta cheese (one 15-ounce container)

1 cup nonfat cottage cheese (one 8-ounce container)

¼ cup loosely packed chopped fresh basil

continued

¼ cup loosely packed
chopped fresh flat-leaf
parsley

1 (12-ounce) package square
wonton wrappers

1½ cups shredded mozzarella
cheese (6 ounces)

Drain any fat from the meat and return the meat to the pan. Add the entire jar of marinara and stir to coat. Set aside.

In a small bowl, stir together the ricotta, cottage cheese, fresh basil, fresh parsley, remaining 1 teaspoon garlic salt, and remaining ¼ teaspoon black pepper.

Arrange 3 wonton wrappers in each prepared muffin cup to create a cup with about an inch of overhang at the top. (I like to place the first wrapper diagonally in the cup with a point down in the bottom and the opposite corner sticking out of the cup on top, then overlap the second and third wrappers so there is no exposed pan visible between wrappers. Basically, as long as you have the inside of the cup covered and there is some overhang on top, you're good to go. Don't overthink it.)

Pinch about 1 teaspoon of shredded mozzarella into the bottom of each wonton cup. Top the mozzarella with a heaping tablespoon of the meat mixture and use a spoon to even it out and squash it down. Scoop an even tablespoon of the ricotta mixture on top of the meat and top that with another pinched teaspoon of mozzarella. The cups should be completely full. Use your fingers to slightly pinch the excess wonton wrappers to wrap the cups up a little on the edges; you should still have most of the mozzarella on top exposed for browning.

Spray the tops of the filled lasagna cups lightly with cooking spray. Bake until the cheese is browned and the wonton wrappers are crisp, 35 to 40 minutes. These are best served hot, but are still yummy at warm room temperature.

Notes

★ I use nonfat cottage cheese because the curds are firmer with less liquid, so it doesn't require straining before mixing with the rest of the ingredients. I also love full-fat ricotta because of how thick and rich it is. Try not to change these two cheeses, if you can help it!

★ When cooking the grated onion, I always put the onion in a cold pan with the oil and heat them together; it seems to keep more moisture in and avoids browning when I'm just trying to cook the onion without getting any color on it.

★ The amount of meat and cheese filling is enough to make about 12 more cups; either use it all up with another package of wonton wrappers (to serve a big group, or freeze some for later), or freeze the fillings to make things quicker the next time you want to make lasagna cups. I find it comes in handy to have prepped fillings at the ready for spontaneous cravings.

★ If you're making a batch of lasagna cups to freeze and reheat later, let the lasagna cups cool completely. Line a baking sheet with parchment paper, set the cooled lasagna cups on the pan, then freeze, uncovered, until solid. Once frozen, throw them in a zip-top bag and freeze for up to 1 month. To reheat, put the cups in a greased muffin tin, cover with aluminum foil, and bake at 350°F for 20 to 30 minutes, until heated through.

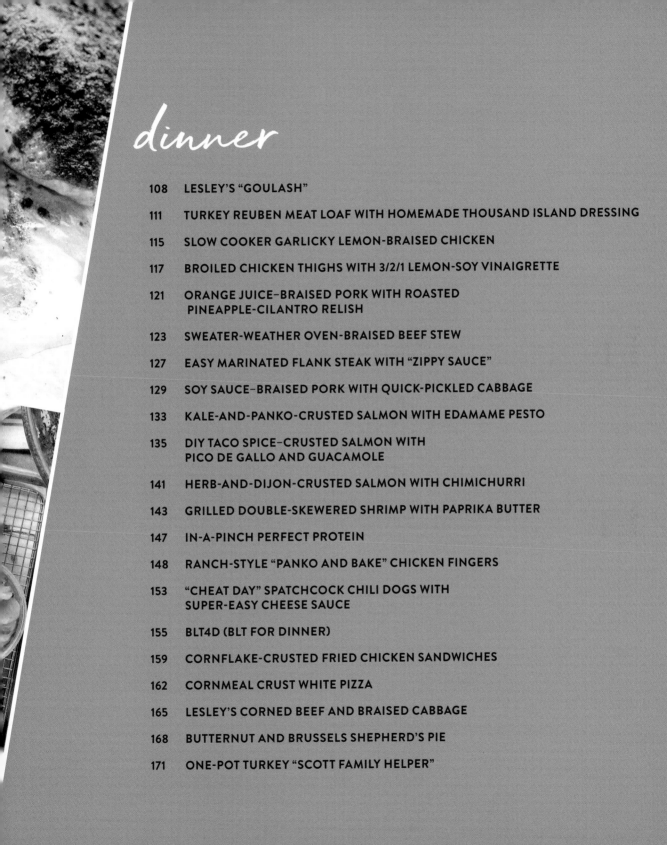

dinner

lesley's "goulash"

Prep Time: 5 minutes | Cook Time: 15 minutes

MAKES 6 SERVINGS

1 pound ground turkey
(93% lean)

1½ teaspoons garlic salt

1 teaspoon ground black
pepper

2 teaspoons olive oil

3 medium zucchini, quartered
lengthwise and sliced into
¼-inch-wide pieces
(4½ cups)

1 large white onion, diced
small (2¾ cups)

2 large garlic cloves, minced
(about 1 tablespoon)

2 (10.5-ounce) cans cream
of mushroom soup

1 tablespoon lemon juice

Who would have thought that after a long career as a chef and a decade and a half of doing TV, I'd be including a recipe from my wife's ex-boyfriend's mother's culinary repertoire in my second cookbook? Not me, that's for sure. But What's-his-name was good for something! In all honesty, this is a truly delicious recipe, and it has been a go-to dish for us for years. Olive absolutely loves it, too (double win). I do have one request: Please don't send the culinary police after me—I know this dish isn't really a "goulash," but that's what I've always called it . . . so goulash will remain.

In a large high-sided skillet or Dutch oven over medium heat, combine the ground turkey, ¾ teaspoon of the garlic salt, and ½ teaspoon of the pepper. Sauté, using a wooden spoon to break the turkey into small bits, until cooked through, 5 to 6 minutes.

Drain the turkey in a strainer to remove any juices.

In the same skillet, combine the oil, zucchini, onion, minced garlic, and remaining ½ teaspoon garlic salt. Cook over medium heat, stirring often, until the zucchini lightens in color and the edges of the onion become translucent, about 5 minutes.

Return the turkey to the skillet, add the cream of mushroom soup and remaining ½ teaspoon pepper, and stir to combine. Bring to a simmer and cook, stirring often, for 2 minutes, or until the mixture is thick and creamy. Stir in the lemon juice. Serve warm in bowls.

Notes

⭑ Make this a more substantial meal by sautéing sliced cremini mushrooms with the onions and zucchini. We always eat it with quinoa (see page 176) and a green salad on the side.

⭑ Don't overcook the zucchini and onions—they should have some bite to them!

turkey reuben meat loaf with homemade thousand island dressing

Prep Time: 10 minutes | Cook Time: 50 minutes | Inactive Time: 30 minutes to overnight

This recipe's history goes back to my first restaurant, Market and Rye. At the time, I was trying to make a leaner, tastier version of meat loaf that was not so heavy on ketchup and gravy. One day while messing around with a food processor—that's my version of working on cars on my day off—I took pastrami, ground turkey (instead of beef), and Swiss cheese and chopped it up with sauerkraut, dill pickle, and the usual spices, and . . . voilà! The Turkey Reuben Meat Loaf was born! Okay, so serving it with homemade Thousand Island dressing definitely doesn't make it particularly healthy, but girlllllllllll, it is *essential* to this dish. Side note: I like to make the meatloaf a day ahead, refrigerate it, then bring it out the next day to slice it and pan-sear it like a steak . . . and then serve it up hot. The Swiss cheese and sauerkraut bits within the meatloaf heat up on the hot griddle and make some culinary magic.

Preheat the oven to 325°F. Spray a 9 x 5-inch loaf pan generously with cooking spray. Cut a piece of parchment paper into a 9-inch-wide strip and lay it in the sprayed pan so that the ends come up and over the long sides of the pan.

In a medium sauté pan, heat 2 tablespoons of the olive oil over medium-high heat. Add the onion and garlic and cook, stirring, for 2 minutes. Add the caraway seeds and cook, stirring continuously, until the caraway is fragrant and the onion is translucent, 2 to 3 minutes.

Transfer the cooked onion mixture to a large bowl. Add the bread crumbs, milk, and egg, and stir to combine. Let the mixture sit for 5 minutes.

In a food processor, combine the pickle, pastrami, and sauerkraut. Pulse the mixture until it has the texture of ground meat. Tear the Swiss cheese slices into the food processor and pulse until the cheese is finely chopped and mixed into

MAKES 4 TO 6 SERVINGS

4 tablespoons olive oil

1 large yellow onion, diced small (about 1½ cups)

1 tablespoon minced garlic

1 tablespoon caraway seeds

¾ cup bread crumbs (I like Italian style, but any type will work)

¼ cup milk

1 egg

1 large dill pickle, chopped (about ¼ cup)

1 (6-ounce) package pastrami, drained

1 cup drained sauerkraut

1 (7-ounce) package sliced Swiss cheese

1 pound ground turkey (85% to 90% lean)

½ teaspoon ground black pepper

Thousand Island Dressing (recipe follows), for serving

continued

the pastrami mixture. Pour this mixture into the bowl with the onion–bread crumb mixture, then add the ground turkey and pepper to the bowl. Mix with your hands until well combined and homogenous.

Press the meat loaf mixture into the prepared pan, making sure it is pressed into the corners and completely even and flat on top. If the overhanging parchment is long enough, fold the ends over the top of the loaf. Bake the meat loaf for 50 minutes. Remove from the oven and let rest in the pan for at least 30 minutes before slicing. Ideally, let it cool at room temperature for 30 minutes to an hour, then let it rest in the refrigerator overnight.

Carefully slide a knife around the edges of the pan and remove the meat loaf. Slice the loaf into 8 even slices a little wider than 1 inch thick. In a large skillet, heat the remaining 2 tablespoons olive oil over medium-high heat. Sear both sides of the meat loaf until well browned, about 4 minutes per side. Serve with the dressing on the side.

Notes

- Cooking meat loaf at a lower temperature for a longer time decreases the amount of fat that leaches out. If you consistently have a problem with meat loaf shrinkage, too high a cooking temperature is surely the culprit.

- This meat loaf is always better the next day. It slices a lot easier and griddles up perfectly—plus, the flavors really meld overnight.

- Obviously, this makes a killer sandwich! Try the seared meat loaf slices on marble rye with the Thousand Island—it will be your new favorite leftover, for sure.

Thousand Island Dressing

MAKES 2¼ CUPS

1 cup mayonnaise

¼ cup minced jarred pepperoncini

2 tablespoons ketchup

2 tablespoons minced dill pickles

2 tablespoons minced capers

¼ teaspoon lemon juice

¼ cup minced red onion

Small pinch of salt

Small pinch of ground black pepper

In a small bowl, whisk together the mayo, pepperoncini, ketchup, pickle, capers, lemon juice, onion, salt, and pepper to combine. I set aside in the fridge until ready to serve. It will keep for up to 2 weeks stored in the fridge in an airtight container.

slow cooker garlicky lemon-braised chicken

Prep Time: 5 minutes | Cook Time: 3 hours 10 minutes

This recipe is for those of you who, like me, love the convenience of the "setting and forgetting" way of preparing a meal. Coming in the door at the end of the day to the aromas (and relief) of a meal that's ready to serve is the best! This recipe is also really, *really* good. The amount of garlic in this dish might seem a bit crazy, but trust me when I say that it's needed (and if you're Italian, this amount is nothing out of the ordinary). When garlic cooks long and slow, it practically turns into candy. I encourage you to use the cheaper cuts of meat such as drums and thighs when making this dish. They retain moisture really well and were born to be slow cooked. Serve the chicken by itself, with polenta, or with my Olive Oil Yukon Gold Mashers (page 208). Thanks to the power of slow cooking and the magic of garlic, you will have an out-of-this-world meal on the table with no fuss or stress (and with all that garlic, no vampires within a 20-mile radius)!

Preheat the oven to 400°F.

Rub the chicken legs with the olive oil. In a small bowl, mix together the onion powder, garlic powder, garlic salt, parsley, and pepper. Sprinkle the spice mixture over both sides of the chicken legs and use your hands to rub it in evenly. Arrange the legs on a wire rack set into a rimmed baking sheet. It's okay if they are touching.

Roast the chicken legs until the skin is dark and crisp and most of the fat has rendered off, 35 to 40 minutes. (They will probably still be raw in the middle; that is okay.)

MAKES 4 TO 6 SERVINGS

6 skin-on whole chicken legs (drumsticks and thighs attached)

2 tablespoons olive oil

2 tablespoons onion powder

3 tablespoons garlic powder

1 tablespoon plus 1 teaspoon garlic salt

1 tablespoon dried parsley

½ teaspoon ground black pepper

Cooking spray, for greasing

1 cup chicken broth

3 lemons, sliced into thin rounds and seeded

50 garlic cloves, peeled (about 1 cup; see Note)

1 large yellow onion, cut in ¼-inch-thick rings

continued

Set your slow cooker to high and spray the insert with cooking spray. Heat the broth in a small saucepan over medium-high heat.

In a large bowl, combine the lemons, garlic cloves, and onion.

Pour the hot broth into your slow cooker. Arrange 3 of the chicken legs in the broth. Top the legs with half the onion-lemon mixture, and arrange the last 3 chicken legs on top of that. Pour the remaining onion-lemon mixture over the chicken and put the lid on the slow cooker. Cook on high for 2½ hours. The chicken will be cooked to the fall-apart stage, and the onions, lemon slices, and garlic will have melted down into a creamy, chunky sauce with the broth. The lemons are totally edible and completely delicious!

Notes

* When applying the spice rub to the chicken legs, try to make sure that the spices don't form clumps on the skin; they could burn and turn bitter in the oven.

* Use leftover chicken from this recipe anywhere you would use roasted or rotisserie chicken. Quesadillas, salads, and soups are all favorites in my family.

* I always use the prepared peeled garlic cloves available at the grocery store, but if you decide to peel your own, you will need 4 or 5 heads of garlic.

* If you don't have a slow cooker and want to cook this on the stovetop, use a heavy pot with a lid like a dutch oven and cook the chicken covered on low heat for 2½ to 3 hours. Check it every 20 to 30 minutes or so and give it a stir to make sure the bottom isn't scorching.

broiled chicken thighs with 3/2/1 lemon-soy vinaigrette

Prep Time: 35 minutes | Cook Time: 12 minutes

Like many other kids from my generation, I was raised on chicken breasts. When I met my wife nine years ago, she pushed me to give the incredible (and super-versatile) chicken *thighs* (the dark meat) a chance! Thighs retain moisture so well, and their flavor is rich and fabulous. These days, we pretty much *only* have dark meat on hand for cooking. Although I use my 3/2/1 Lemon-Soy Vinaigrette for all sorts of things, including salads, I originally came up with it as a marinade for chicken thighs. These can be eaten hot, thrown into a stir-fry, chopped up cold for a salad, sliced up for a sandwich, or eaten on the go caveman-style (hunk of meat in your bare hand). You'll never regret making these on a Monday to help stretch your meals through the whole week.

Trim any excess fat and bits of skin from the chicken thighs. Toss them with 1 teaspoon of the garlic salt and place them in an 8-inch square baking dish.

In a small bowl, whisk together the olive oil, lemon juice, soy sauce, and remaining ½ teaspoon garlic salt. Pour half the dressing over the chicken in the baking dish and stir to coat the meat. Set aside the rest of the dressing. Press the chicken down so that the dressing is in contact with all the meat and can start to infuse it with flavor. Let the thighs marinate at room temperature for 30 minutes.

Preheat the broiler.

MAKES 4 SERVINGS

2 pounds boneless, skinless chicken thighs

1½ teaspoons garlic salt

¾ cup olive oil

½ cup lemon juice

¼ cup soy sauce

continued

broiled chicken thighs with 3/2/1 lemon-soy vinaigrette, continued

Arrange the chicken thighs on a wire rack fitted into a rimmed baking sheet. Brush them with some of the leftover dressing and broil for 12 to 15 minutes, brushing them with more dressing about halfway through. The edges should be dark brown and charred, with sizzling golden brown everywhere else. (You can also get great results on a grill.)

Note

★ I like to make a large batch of 3/2/1 dressing (see the recipe on page 63 for a larger batch) and keep it in the fridge. Just be sure to throw out any dressing that you've marinated raw chicken in, or dipped a brush or tongs into after using them to touch raw chicken. Bacteria from the raw chicken could be transferred to the dressing, making it unsafe to eat.

orange juice–braised pork with roasted pineapple-cilantro relish

Prep Time: 10 minutes | Cook Time: 3½ hours

This braise uses orange juice to flavor and tenderize a less expensive cut of pork (the shoulder, otherwise known as the pork butt) and is what I like to call a "set it and forget it" dish. You might think the orange flavor would be overwhelming, but when it simmers and cooks down with the oregano, garlic, and onion it becomes melt-in-your-mouth *perfection!* Served with the pineapple-cilantro relish, the flavor explosion is beyond words, so please don't skip it—it is essential. Since, like most braises, this dish is better the next day, a great and simple idea for the leftovers is to fry the pork in a pan and make carnitas quesadillas. Serve them with the relish on top, and it is leftover heaven. These two-for-one meals are what so often saves our family in the busiest of weeks. Here's another culinary lifesaver—grab hold!

COOK THE PORK: Cut the excess fat from the pork shoulder and cut the meat into large 3-inch cubes. Toss the cubes of pork in a large bowl with the salt, pepper, and oregano. In a large braising pan or Dutch oven, heat the olive oil over high heat. Add the seasoned pork and cook, undisturbed, for 5 minutes to get a nice brown sear. Stir the pork cubes and sear the other side until browned, 4 to 5 minutes. Reduce the heat to low and add the orange juice, broth, onion, garlic, jalapeño, and bay leaf. Stir to combine and use a wooden spoon to loosen any bits of pork stuck to the bottom of the pan. Put the cilantro on top of the braising mixture, cover the pot with a tight-fitting lid, and cook until the meat is fork-tender, about 3 hours.

MAKES 4 TO 6 SERVINGS

For the pork

2½ pounds pork shoulder

1 tablespoon kosher salt

1½ teaspoons ground black pepper

1 tablespoon dried oregano

3 tablespoons olive oil

2 cups orange juice

1 cup chicken broth

1 onion, quartered

2 garlic cloves, chopped

½ jalapeño, chopped

1 bay leaf

½ bunch cilantro

1½ tablespoons cold unsalted butter, cubed

continued

orange juice–braised pork with roasted pineapple-cilantro relish, continued

For the relish

½ red onion, diced small

1 large jalapeño, seeded and minced (about ¼ cup)

2 tablespoons lemon juice

⅛ teaspoon garlic salt

¾ teaspoon kosher salt

⅛ teaspoon ground black pepper

Pinch of red pepper flakes

¼ cup olive oil

½ fresh pineapple, peeled, cored, and diced (about 4 cups)

1 teaspoon minced fresh ginger

1 teaspoon minced garlic

½ bunch scallions, thinly sliced (about ½ cup loosely packed)

¼ bunch cilantro, coarsely chopped (about ½ cup loosely packed)

Use tongs to remove and discard the cilantro stems (the leaves will have fallen off and become part of the sauce). Use a slotted spoon to remove the pork from the liquid and set aside in a bowl. Increase the heat under the pot to high and boil the broth until it has reduced to about 1½ cups. Take the pot off the heat and whisk in the butter. Return the pork to the pot and stir to coat all the meat with the sauce, being careful not to let the pork fall apart too much.

Preheat the broiler to 500°F. Line a baking sheet with parchment paper or aluminum foil.

WHILE THE PORK COOKS, MAKE THE RELISH: In a large bowl, stir together the onion, jalapeño, lemon juice, garlic salt, salt, black pepper, red pepper flakes, and 2 tablespoons of the olive oil. In a separate bowl, toss the diced pineapple with the remaining 2 tablespoons olive oil, ginger, and garlic. Spread the pineapple on the prepared baking sheet and broil until the pineapple caramelizes and turns dark brown at the edges, about 15 minutes. Let the pineapple cool for 10 minutes, then fold it into the onion-jalapeño mixture. Add the scallions and cilantro and fold to combine.

Serve the pork with the pineapple relish.

Notes

⭐ Don't add the scallions and cilantro to the relish until you are about to serve. If the herbs sit with the lemon and pineapple for too long, they will start to turn brown from the acid.

⭐ Avoid using Maui Gold pineapples, if you can; they have a higher sugar content and will break down to mush when you roast them.

sweater-weather
oven-braised beef stew

Prep Time: 15 minutes | Cook Time: 2½ to 3 hours

If you love to stretch your dollar, this braised beef is for you. Inexpensive cuts of meat like the knuckle meat, chuck roll, or shoulder clod are perfect for this recipe. In order to have the meat prepped and ready any time I'm in the mood for this stew, I dice it, bag it up, and freeze it (your butcher can also dice it up for you if you'd prefer). You can actually make this quintessential comfort food any time of year, sweater or no sweater. I also like to change the kind of wine that I pair with this meal based on the time of year. For example, pair it with a cabernet for winter, a pinot for spring, or a chardonnay for summer! This stew freezes well, so you can always have a few servings ready for a last-minute heat-up.

Preheat the oven to 375°F.

In a large Dutch oven, heat 2 tablespoons of the canola oil over high heat.

In a large bowl, toss together the beef cubes, flour, salt, and pepper until well coated. Working in four batches, cook the meat until browned on all sides, about 5 minutes per batch; add an additional 2 tablespoons canola oil to the pot before each batch. Transfer the browned meat to a large plate.

MAKES 6 TO 8 SERVINGS

½ cup canola oil

4 pounds chuck roast, cut into 1-inch cubes

3 tablespoons all-purpose flour

1 tablespoon salt

¼ teaspoon freshly ground black pepper

1 (6-ounce) can tomato paste

1 (750-ml) bottle Pinot Noir

3 cups beef broth

1 large yellow onion, diced (2¾ cups)

2 celery stalks, diced (1 cup)

8 ounces cremini mushrooms, sliced (2 cups)

4 garlic cloves, minced (1 tablespoon)

6 sprigs thyme

4 sprigs parsley, plus more for serving

1 bay leaf

1 pound baby potatoes

1 pound baby carrots

1 cup frozen pearl onions

1 tablespoon apple cider vinegar

continued

sweater-weather oven-braised beef stew, continued

Carefully drain any excess oil from the Dutch oven, reduce the heat to medium-high, and return all the meat to the pot, along with any juices that have accumulated on the plate. Add the tomato paste and cook, stirring continuously, until the meat is coated and the paste has thickened and begins to toast, 1 to 2 minutes. Add the wine, broth, diced onion, celery, mushrooms, garlic, thyme, parsley, and bay leaf and bring to a simmer. Cover the Dutch oven with a lid and place it in the oven. Braise for 1½ hours. Add the potatoes, carrots, and pearl onions to the Dutch oven, stir, and braise until the vegetables are fork-tender, about 1 hour more.

Using tongs, remove the herbs and bay leaf. Stir in the vinegar and serve with a sprinkling of chopped parsley.

Note

★ Although this recipe has a full bottle of wine in it, all the alcohol cooks off, and it absolutely does not end up tasting like wine. My entire family (including little Olive) loves it, and that's why it's such a big recipe; I freeze half in quart-size zip-top bags for easy reheating.

easy marinated flank steak with "zippy sauce"

Prep Time: 30 minutes | Cook Time: 20 minutes

Let me tell you a bit about my in-laws. My mother-in-law is the queen of marinades . . . she marinates *everything!* Just like her, I love a good marinade, but *unlike* her, I love some spicy heat in mine. Now, about my father-in-law. Flank steak is his favorite thing to cook, especially on the grill, but when his daughter married a chef, he started questioning his grilling skills. Michael, trust me: You are a fabulous grill master (now it's in writing)—I'm here to tell you that if you know how to do something well, never question it! Here's my stick-to-what-I-know spin on my mother-in-law's marinade, and I hope you love it. If you prefer a spicier flavor, add more jalapeños. By the way, the "zippy sauce" I serve on the side can go on *everything.* (Maybe not on ice cream—but prove me wrong!) It's also a great vegan option to add interest to any side dish. It goes beautifully on tofu, eggplant, or quinoa, and I'm sure you'll find even more killer combos for its use.

MARINATE THE STEAK: In a gallon-size zip-top bag, combine the olive oil, honey, vinegar, pepper, salt, smoked paprika, and chili powder. Put the steak in the bag, seal it, and massage it a little to get the meat fully covered with marinade. Marinate in the refrigerator for at least 30 minutes or up to 2 hours.

MAKE THE SAUCE: In a food processor, combine the jalapeños with the lemon juice and pulse to finely chop, then transfer to a medium bowl.

In the food processor, combine the arugula, mint, parsley, garlic, cumin, salt, pepper, and olive oil and pulse until the mixture looks like pesto. Transfer this mixture to the bowl with the jalapeños and mix it all together. Transfer to an airtight container and store in the fridge until serving time. (The longer the zippy sauce sits, the more the flavors meld and bloom, making it more delicious.)

MAKES 4 SERVINGS

For the marinated steak

¼ cup olive oil

3 tablespoons honey

2 tablespoons rice vinegar

1 teaspoon ground black pepper

1½ teaspoons kosher salt

½ teaspoon smoked paprika

½ teaspoon chili powder

1 (1½- to 2-pound) flank steak

For the zippy sauce

2 jalapeños, seeded, if desired, and coarsely chopped

Juice of 1 lemon

1 cup arugula

½ cup fresh mint leaves

½ cup fresh parsley leaves

1 garlic clove, peeled

1 teaspoon ground cumin

1 teaspoon kosher salt

1 teaspoon ground black pepper

½ cup olive oil

continued

Heat a grill until it's nice and hot. Carefully place the marinated flank steak on the grill. Cook, uncovered, for 7 to 8 minutes. You want to really caramelize that honey in the marinade and get some nice dark grill marks. Using tongs, carefully flip the steak and cook for 7 to 8 minutes more for medium-rare (a meat thermometer inserted into the thickest part of the steak should read 130°F).

Transfer the steak to a large cutting board and let it rest for 15 minutes so the juices redistribute.

Then cut the meat into thin strips against the grain for maximum tenderness. Spoon the zippy sauce over the steak and enjoy!

Note

★ When cooking meats, a good rule of thumb is to rest the meat for the same amount of time that it cooked to ensure that the juices have enough time to redistribute and allow the proteins to relax.

soy sauce–braised pork with quick-pickled cabbage

Prep Time: 10 minutes | Cook Time: 1 hour 30 minutes

Lesley is of Chinese heritage on her mother's side, so it's always been important for us to acknowledge and celebrate this, especially for Olive. This pork dish is one of the recipes that Lesley has been cooking from the book of her mom's home recipes—a collection gathered over the years. Two things that are not original to this recipe are my addition of butter to finish the sauce (I couldn't help myself—I love how butter makes the sauce glossy and rich) and the pickled cabbage. The acidity in the cabbage cuts through the rich saltiness of the pork nicely and is a great crunchy side to complement this super-scrumptious pork!

MAKE THE PORK: Trim the excess fat and connective tissue from the pork shoulder and cut the meat into large, 2- to 3-inch chunks. Rinse the pork pieces under cold running water and put them in a Dutch oven or small stockpot. Add cold water to cover the pork by about 2 inches. Bring to a boil over high heat, then boil for 10 minutes. Turn the heat off and skim off the foam floating on top. Using a small measuring cup or handled cup, remove 1½ cups of water from the pot and set it aside. Add the sherry, soy sauce, brown sugar, ginger, and garlic to the pot and stir to combine. The pork should still be completely submerged in liquid. If it isn't, add more of the cooking liquid back to the pot until the pork is completely covered. Bring the liquid back to a boil, then reduce the heat to low and simmer the pork, uncovered, until just fork-tender, about 1½ hours. As it cooks, the liquid will reduce, so be sure to give the pork a good stir every 10 to 15 minutes to keep it moist.

MAKES 4 TO 6 SERVINGS

For the pork

1 (2½- to 3-pound) pork shoulder

4 to 8 cups cold water

2 cups dry sherry

¾ cup soy sauce

¼ cup lightly packed light brown sugar

3 tablespoons minced fresh ginger

1 tablespoon minced garlic

2 tablespoons molasses

3 tablespoons unsalted butter

continued

soy sauce–braised pork with quick-pickled cabbage, continued

For the cabbage

¾ cup small-diced red onion

1 large jalapeño, minced
(about ¼ cup)

3 tablespoons lemon juice

1 tablespoon granulated sugar

1 tablespoon rice vinegar

½ teaspoon salt

¼ teaspoon garlic salt

¼ teaspoon ground black
pepper

1 small or ½ large head
green cabbage, shredded
(about 6 cups)

¼ teaspoon toasted
sesame oil

Turn the heat off and add the molasses. Taste the cooking liquid; if it tastes watery, remove the pork, bring the liquid to a boil, and cook until it reduces and has a strong soy sauce flavor without being too salty, about 5 to 10 minutes. Turn the heat off and add the butter, whisking continuously to emulsify. If you removed the pork, return it to the pot with the sauce and stir to coat.

WHILE THE PORK IS COOKING, QUICK-PICKLE THE CABBAGE: In a large bowl, mix together the onion, jalapeño, lemon juice, sugar, vinegar, salt, and pepper. Let it sit for 5 minutes to macerate so the flavors can meld and mellow. Add the cabbage and sesame oil and work the dressing into the cabbage with your hands, massaging, massaging the cabbage until it slightly softens and starts to absorb the dressing, 2 to 3 minutes. Cover and set aside until the pork is ready to eat.

Lesley likes to serve the pork and pickled cabbage with scallions over brown rice. (It's even better the next day!)

Notes

★ The water quantity is variable based on the size and shape of your cooking vessel. The most important thing is that the pork is covered with liquid while cooking. When the pork is done cooking, be sure to taste the cooking liquid and adjust the seasoning in the seasoning in the rest of the recipe according to your taste.

★ I like a punchy sauce that coats the meat, so I reduce the cooking liquid by boiling it for a few minutes before adding the butter.

★ For the quick pickle, you can use a mix of purple and green cabbage, or all purple, if you like. You can even add some shredded or grated carrots to the mix for a little more sweetness and color.

kale-and-panko-crusted salmon with edamame pesto

Prep Time: 5 minutes | Cook Time: 40 minutes

I love this salmon dish because it's a protein and a veggie all in one! The kale crust acts as a moisture barrier, keeping the fish nice and moist as it bakes, and also becomes a delicious way to have greens. The pesto is so flavorful and packed with protein from the edamame.

The Dijon doesn't come across as mustardy-tasting at all. It adds a wonderful bit of acidity to the rich fatty salmon, and is the perfect way to get the kale-and-panko crust to stick.

COOK THE SALMON: Preheat the oven to 275°F. Line a baking sheet with parchment paper.

Place the salmon skin-side down on the prepared baking sheet. Make sure there are no stray pin bones by feeling up and down the salmon with your fingertips. Remove any bones you find with tweezers. Tuck the skinny tail end under to even out the width and thickness of the fish to ensure even baking.

Spread the mustard over the surface of the salmon using a rubber spatula or the back of a spoon.

In a food processor, combine the kale, spinach, panko, dill, parsley, olive oil, garlic salt, and pepper. Pulse until the mixture is finely chopped.

Pour the kale-panko mixture on top of the salmon and spread it evenly over the surface of the fish with your hands, then use your hands to press it against the fish, packing it down.

MAKES 6 TO 8 SERVINGS

For the salmon

1 (2½-pound) side of salmon, brought to room temperature

¼ cup Dijon mustard

1 cup packed fresh chopped kale

1 cup packed baby spinach

¾ cup panko bread crumbs

2 tablespoons fresh dill

2 tablespoons chopped fresh parsley

2 tablespoons olive oil

1 teaspoon garlic salt

½ teaspoon ground black pepper

1 lemon, cut into wedges

1 tablespoon Maldon sea salt

continued

For the pesto

1 cup frozen cooked shelled edamame beans, thawed

1 cup loosely packed basil leaves (from about 1 bunch)

¼ cup vegetable broth

2 to 4 tablespoons coconut milk

1 tablespoon lemon juice

1 tablespoon vegetable oil

1 teaspoon minced garlic

½ teaspoon minced fresh ginger

1½ teaspoons toasted sesame oil

½ teaspoon fish sauce

⅛ teaspoon red pepper flakes

Bake the salmon for about 40 minutes. You can sneak a peek at the thickest part of the salmon with a paring knife: the flesh should be light-medium pink and moist when the fish is ready. Do not continue cooking the fish until it flakes; it will be dry by then. Finish the salmon with a squeeze of lemon juice and sprinkle with the Maldon salt.

MAKE THE PESTO: In a food processor, combine the edamame, basil, broth, 2 tablespoons of the coconut milk, the lemon juice, vegetable oil, garlic, ginger, sesame oil, fish sauce, and red pepper flakes. Pulse until the pesto is creamy yet still a little chunky. If you'd like it thinner, add a little more coconut milk and/or broth.

To serve (warm or room temp is great), use a spatula to gently cut portions of fish and lift them off the skin. Spoon some pesto over each portion and enjoy!

diy taco spice–crusted salmon with pico de gallo and guacamole

Prep Time: 30 minutes | Cook Time: 40 minutes

I'm a guy who was raised on food made with seasoning packets (I'm sure many of you can relate!). Ranch dressing, sloppy Joe seasoning—you name it, we had a packet for it. We made (and stretched) so many meals that way. This recipe features my own DIY take on taco spice, used here to season a side of salmon—although it can also go on pork, shrimp, beef, or tofu. Call it "Tinker Bell's fairy dust" if it will get the kids to eat a full meal! This creation was born out of necessity (or was it hunger?). My wife and family members seriously love my guacamole and pico de gallo, and one day, I was trying to find a light and simple protein to go with them and found myself with a side of salmon and a load of tortillas in the fridge. This resulting salmon dish makes an amazing dinner, but is also screaming to be taken to a party or served as a brunch or a light afternoon lunch.

Preheat the oven to 275°F. Line a baking sheet with parchment paper.

MAKE THE TACO SEASONING: In a small bowl, combine the cumin, ground chili powder, oregano, garlic salt, onion powder, paprika, cayenne, and black pepper. Pour the mixture into a medium sauté pan and toast over low heat, stirring frequently to prevent burning, until the spices become super-fragrant and turn a little darker in color, about 5 minutes. Immediately pour the hot spice mix onto a plate and let it cool off.

Place the side of salmon skin-side down on the prepared baking sheet. Make sure there are no stray pin bones by feeling up and down the flesh with your fingertips; remove any bones you find with tweezers. Tuck the skinny tail end under to even out the width and thickness and to ensure even baking.

In a small bowl, mix the mayo and lime juice together. Using a rubber spatula or

MAKES 6 TO 8 SERVINGS

For the homemade taco seasoning

2 tablespoons ground cumin

2 tablespoons chili powder

1 tablespoon dried oregano

1 tablespoon garlic salt

1½ teaspoons onion powder

2¼ teaspoons paprika

¾ teaspoon cayenne pepper

½ teaspoon ground black pepper

For the salmon

1 (2½-pound) side of salmon, brought to room temperature

¼ cup mayonnaise

1 tablespoon lime juice

1 lime, cut into wedges

continued

diy taco spice–crusted salmon with pico de gallo and guacamole, continued

the back of a spoon, spread the mayo over the salmon, covering all the pink flesh. Sprinkle ¼ cup of the taco seasoning over the mayo-coated salmon, coating it as evenly as you can. (Store any remaining taco seasoning in an airtight container at room temperature for up to a year.)

Bake the salmon for about 40 minutes. You can sneak a peek at the thickest part of the salmon with a paring knife: the flesh should be light-medium pink and moist when the salmon is ready. Do not continue cooking the fish until it flakes; it will be dry by then. Finish the salmon with a squeeze of lime juice.

MAKE THE PICO DE GALLO AND GUACAMOLE: Set up two medium bowls side by side. Put the red onion in each bowl, along with the minced jalapeño, lemon juice, salt, and garlic salt. Mix each bowl to combine the ingredients, and let them sit for at least 5 minutes while you chop the tomatoes (you should have about 3 cups) and pit and peel the avocados (save one of the pits for storing the guacamole). For the pico de gallo, add the chopped tomatoes to the onion mixture and toss to combine. Add the cilantro last, folding it gently to avoid mashing and bruising it up. For the guacamole, add the avocados to the onion mixture. Use a wooden spoon to mash and chop up the avocados as you mix. Don't overmix or mash them too much; this guacamole is meant to be chunky and thick enough to break a chip. Add the cilantro to the guacamole and gently fold it in.

Toast the tortillas by holding them with metal tongs and quickly passing them over a stovetop burner (gas or electric both work fine) set to medium-low heat. Toast each side until light brown spots start to appear and the tortillas become soft and pliable, 30 to 45 seconds per side.

Serve the salmon with the freshly toasted corn tortillas, the pico de gallo, and the guacamole.

For the pico de gallo

½ medium red onion, minced (about ¾ cup)

1 large jalapeño, half the seeds removed, minced (about ¼ cup)

2 tablespoons fresh lemon juice

½ teaspoon kosher salt

⅛ teaspoon garlic salt

5 medium tomatoes

½ bunch cilantro, coarsely chopped (about ⅓ cup)

For the guacamole

½ medium red onion, minced (about ¾ cup)

1 large jalapeño, half the seeds removed, minced (about ¼ cup)

2½ tablespoons fresh lemon juice

½ teaspoon kosher salt

¼ teaspoon garlic salt

4 medium-large avocados

½ bunch cilantro, coarsely chopped (about ⅓ cup)

12 taco-size corn tortillas, for serving

continued

diy taco spice–crusted salmon with pico de gallo and guacamole, continued

Notes

- For the pico and guacamole, it's super-important to let the lemon juice and salt sit with the grated onion and jalapeño before adding the rest of the ingredients. It helps to mellow the harshness of the raw onion and starts to break down the oils in the jalapeño, resulting in more melded flavors.

- I always use fresh lemons and squeeze them just before using in this recipe. Frozen lemon juice or juice from concentrate won't be the same, I guarantee. If your lemons seem underripe and hard, try microwaving them for 10 to 20 seconds, then roll them under your palm to release the juice from the fibers inside before cutting them open.

- If you'll be storing the guacamole in the fridge, save one of the avocado seeds and pop it into the guacamole, then press plastic wrap directly against the surface of the guacamole, covering it completely, to avoid browning.

- If you like your pico de gallo and guacamole spicy, leave in more of the jalapeño seeds (or remove all the seeds, if you prefer things totally mild).

- No need to go crazy picking the leaves off the stems before chopping cilantro; give the whole bunch a good rinse and shake, then chop it from the top down, stopping when you reach the thicker stems.

- Save the extra taco seasoning for Taco Tuesday or use it in my Super Veggie Chili con Corny (page 75).

herb-and-dijon-crusted salmon with chimichurri

Prep Time: 20 minutes | Cook Time: 40 minutes

You're thinking, "Really, Ryan? Three salmon recipes in one book?" Yep. Guilty as charged. But salmon is delicious, healthy, and very economical, and if you cook it my way, it doesn't put out that aroma that screams "I'm cooking fish!" I've made this dish for over a decade, and it's one of my number one requested and downloaded recipes. After it is cooked, let it rest until it is at room temperature and then serve it on a platter with lettuce cups, quinoa, or whatever your heart desires. It can be a whole meal by itself or a great accompaniment to other dishes. Salmon does not have a specific region or cuisine that it calls its own, so this accommodating fish can be served with *anything*. My chimichurri and all of the wonderful herbs in the salmon crust will appeal to all tastes. It will surely be a *swimming* success.

COOK THE SALMON: Preheat the oven to 275°F. Line a baking sheet with parchment paper.

Place the salmon skin-side down on the prepared baking sheet. Make sure there are no stray pin bones by feeling up and down the flesh with your fingertips; remove any bones you find with tweezers. Tuck the skinny tail end under to even out the width and thickness and to ensure even baking. Sprinkle the Old Bay seasoning evenly over the salmon.

In a food processor, combine the jalapeño, shallot, parsley, dill, lemon juice, mustard, salt, pepper, Tabasco, and olive oil. Pulse until the herbs, shallot, and jalapeño are chopped fine and the mixture resembles pesto.

MAKES 6 TO 8 SERVINGS

For the salmon

1 (2½-pound) side of salmon, brought to room temperature

1½ teaspoons Old Bay seasoning

1 medium jalapeño, coarsely chopped (include the seeds if you like it spicy)

1 medium shallot, coarsely chopped

¼ cup coarsely chopped fresh parsley

¼ cup fresh dill

3 tablespoons lemon juice

2 tablespoons Dijon mustard

2 teaspoons salt

1½ teaspoons ground black pepper

2 dashes of Tabasco sauce

¼ cup olive oil

continued

For the chimichurri

Leaves from ½ bunch parsley, chopped

1 tablespoon dried oregano

1 teaspoon smoked paprika

½ shallot, minced

Zest and juice of ½ lemon

½ cup extra-virgin olive oil

½ teaspoon salt

¼ teaspoon ground black pepper

1 tablespoon red wine vinegar

Pour the entire herb mixture over the salmon, and use a spatula or spoon to spread it evenly over the pink flesh, covering it completely.

Bake the salmon for 35 minutes. Then turn the broiler on and broil the salmon for 5 minutes, just until the herb-mustard crust starts to caramelize and sizzle.

MAKE THE CHIMICHURRI: In a food processor, combine the parsley, oregano, paprika, shallot, lemon zest, lemon juice, olive oil, salt, and pepper and pulse until the herbs are finely chopped. Add the vinegar just before serving.

To serve the salmon, scoop portions off of the skin and serve each portion with some of the chimichurri.

Note

★ You can make a larger batch of chimichurri and store it in the fridge (without the vinegar) for up to a week, then add the vinegar just before serving. Otherwise, the acid in the vinegar can make the herbs brown faster than usual.

grilled double-skewered shrimp with paprika butter

Prep Time: 15 minutes | Cook Time: 5 minutes

Meals of shrimp, lobster, or other seafood were infrequent and considered "special" in my household when I was growing up. We all loved seafood, but the price tag was pretty impractical. But my dad, Danny, loves shrimp so much, my family dubbed him the "shrimp king," so I created this recipe for him. Instead of sautéing the shrimp in a pan, here's an easy way to grill them. Shrimp coil up quickly when put on heat, and then they fall through the grate (bringing out a string of expletives from me). But if you use the double-skewer method, it becomes quite easy to grill and flip these guys. The time spent skewering the shrimp is absolutely worth it! It is a far better alternative to losing half your meal to the red-hot briquettes. Here's to my amazing dad—this one's for you! #NoFathersDayCardNeeded

MARINATE THE SHRIMP: In a medium bowl, combine the salt, lemon pepper, garlic powder, and lemon zest. Toss the shrimp in the spice mixture until completely coated. Cover the bowl and marinate in the refrigerator for at least 10 minutes or up to 1 hour.

MAKE THE SAUCE: In a small saucepan, combine the wine and onion. Bring to a simmer over medium heat and cook for 2 minutes to cook off the alcohol. Add the butter, garlic, garlic powder, lemon pepper, paprika, and Tabasco. Turn the heat off and stir the sauce for 1 to 2 minutes, until the butter is softened and almost completely melted. Set aside while you grill the shrimp.

Preheat a grill to medium-high or heat a grill pan over medium-high heat. Spray the grill grates or pan with cooking spray.

MAKES 4 SERVINGS

For the shrimp

1½ teaspoons salt

1 teaspoon lemon pepper

1 teaspoon garlic powder

1 medium lemon, zested and cut into wedges

32 jumbo shrimp, peeled (tails left attached) and deveined

Cooking spray

For the sauce

½ cup dry white wine

1 tablespoon finely chopped onion

¾ cup (1½ sticks) butter, cut into 1-tablespoon pieces

3 garlic cloves, minced

½ teaspoon garlic powder

½ teaspoon lemon pepper

½ teaspoon paprika

6 dashes of Tabasco sauce

Fresh parsley, for garnish

continued

Lay the marinated shrimp flat on their sides on a baking sheet, arranged in columns of four. Thread one skewer through the thickest part of 4 shrimp, then thread another skewer through their tail ends. Repeat to double-skewer all the shrimp.

Grill the shrimp and lemon wedges for 2 to 3 minutes on each side, until the shrimp are completely pink.

While the shrimp are hot, brush them with the paprika butter, squeeze the grilled lemon over them, and garnish with parsley if using. Serve immediately or at warm room temp (so that the butter doesn't congeal).

Note

★ If you're using wooden skewers, soak them in water for at least an hour before loading them with shrimp and grilling; this will prevent the skewers from burning.

in-a-pinch perfect protein

Prep Time: 2 minutes | Cook Time: 6 minutes

Having some sort of cooked protein in our refrigerator (a pound or more) is a rule that my wife and I live by. It can save us in a pinch on super-busy days and gives us a healthy option to feed our daughter that is not battered and fried (like many convenience foods for toddlers). This recipe is Lesley's creation, and it's a superhero in the versatility department. It is fabulous in tacos or a lasagna, stuffed in a bell pepper, or tossed on top of a salad! It's a time-saver and a kind of weeknight-dinner "insurance policy." I have also been known to eat it by the spoonful, straight out of the fridge—no heating necessary. Get in my belly!

MAKES 4 SERVINGS

1 tablespoon olive oil

1 pound lean ground turkey or beef

2 tablespoons lemon juice

1 tablespoon liquid aminos or low-sodium soy sauce

½ teaspoon garlic salt

3 tablespoons thinly sliced scallions

In a medium skillet, heat the olive oil over medium-high heat. Add the ground meat and sauté, stirring frequently with a wooden spoon and breaking up the meat as it cooks, until any liquid that has leached out of the meat has evaporated and the meat is fully cooked, 4 to 5 minutes. (I like to break my ground meat up a fair amount so that there is more surface area to soak up the lemon and aminos.)

Add the lemon juice, aminos, and garlic salt and stir well to combine and coat all the bits of turkey. Turn the heat off to prevent the lemon juice and aminos from burning. Sprinkle the scallions on top. Serve as desired or pack it up in airtight containers and store in the fridge for up to 1 week.

Notes

* When I brown ground turkey, I don't actually cook it until brown. I cook it until the turkey is cooked through and any liquids that have come out of it start to evaporate. Turkey is so lean, true browning would overcook it and make it dry.

* If you're using ground beef, stick to a leaner blend (at least 90% lean).

* If you don't have access to liquid aminos, try using low-sodium soy sauce instead, or use half the amount of regular soy sauce.

ranch-style "panko and bake" chicken fingers

Prep Time: 10 minutes | Cook Time: 25 minutes | Inactive Time: 25 minutes

MAKES 4 SERVINGS

For the chicken

6 boneless, skinless chicken thighs

½ cup milk

1 tablespoon vinegar

1 tablespoon plus 1 teaspoon Ranch Powder (recipe follows)

Cooking spray

2 cups panko bread crumbs

¼ cup olive oil

For the ranch dipping sauce

¾ cup mayonnaise

½ cup sour cream

¼ cup milk

1½ tablespoons Ranch Powder (recipe follows)

2 teaspoons vinegar

Three things have not changed in my family in the forty years I have been on this earth: ranch dressing, my mom's spaghetti sauce, and her chocolate chip cookies. One thing I can count on when visiting my parents in Bend, Oregon, is that there will always be a big jar of ranch dressing (made with a helping hand from a Hidden Valley packet) ready for us. So, here's a recipe inspired by my mom and adapted for *my* little family by incorporating ranch dressing into baked chicken fingers. I've put ranch in both the marinade and the breading of the chicken fingers, so they are *clearly* meant to be dipped in it, too, right? This will be a go-to meal for your family right away. I guarantee that any kid (or kid at heart) will love it.

MAKE THE CHICKEN: Trim the excess fat and bits of skin from the chicken thighs and cut each thigh into 3 or 4 strips.

In a large, shallow dish, whisk together the milk, vinegar, and 1 tablespoon of the ranch powder. Add the chicken pieces and mix well, making sure the chicken is completely coated with the marinade. Cover with plastic wrap and let sit at room temperature for 20 minutes.

Preheat the oven to 425°F. Line a baking sheet with parchment paper or aluminum foil and spray with cooking spray.

In a large zip-top bag, combine the panko, olive oil, and remaining 1 teaspoon ranch powder. Close the bag and shake it very well, making sure the bread crumbs are all coated with the seasoning and oil.

continued

Drain the marinated chicken in a strainer, discarding all the marinade. Take 4 to 6 chicken strips and toss them into the bag with the panko mixture. Seal the bag and shake it up, using your hands to gently press the bread crumbs against the chicken to fully coat. Put the coated chicken pieces on the prepared baking sheet, making sure to leave at least ½ inch of space between them. Repeat to coat the remaining chicken.

Bake the chicken until cooked through and golden brown, about 25 minutes.

MEANWHILE, MAKE THE DIPPING SAUCE: In a small bowl, combine the mayo, sour cream, milk, ranch powder, and vinegar. Whisk thoroughly, then store the dip in the fridge until the chicken is ready.

Serve the chicken fingers with the ranch dip alongside.

DIY Ranch Powder

MAKES 1½ CUPS

¼ cup garlic salt

¼ cup dried parsley

3 tablespoons onion powder

2½ tablespoons dried chives

1½ tablespoons dried dill

1 teaspoon ground black pepper

¼ teaspoon paprika

Combine all the ingredients in a food processor. Pulse until the herbs are finely chopped and the powder is well mixed. Store in an airtight container at room temperature for up to 1 year.

Notes

* I mix my ranch powder in a food processor to get the dried herbs nice and pulverized and to make sure the mixture is totally homogenous. If you like to see the whole dried parsley leaves and chives, go ahead and mix it by hand. Just be sure to mix it each time you use it; some spices may settle more than others.

* Use whatever vinegar you have in the house. I always have apple cider vinegar around, so that's usually my choice, but this recipe works with almost anything. (Rice vinegar will be too sweet, and red wine vinegar will make it pink, so stay away from those two.)

* I don't coat all the chicken in the bread crumbs at once because I don't want the bread crumbs to turn soggy from the marinade clinging to the chicken. Doing it in batches helps to ensure that each chicken strip gets well coated with plenty of dry, crispy bread crumbs.

* As the ranch dip sits in the fridge, it thickens, the flavor gets better, and the spices bloom. I like to make a double recipe and store it in the fridge for up to 2 weeks. It's amazing with pizza!

* Ranch powder is great as a dry marinade for grilled veggies, or as the salt and seasoning for a homemade vinaigrette (no mayo or sour cream required!). I also like to sprinkle it on shrimp before sautéing for a yummy herbaceous take on scampi, or on buttered baked potatoes or even popcorn.

* If you want to make this gluten-free, swap in gluten-free panko without worry—it will be delicious!

"cheat day" spatchcock chili dogs with super-easy cheese sauce

Prep Time: 5 minutes | Cook Time: 2 to 3 hours

Ninety percent of the time when I'm writing recipes, they're inspired by *good* memories from past food experiences. This is the exception. I have eaten some really bad hot dogs through the years—stale buns, cold meat, uninteresting condiments. These chili dogs—the perfect combination of sweet (the bun), snappy (the grilled hot dog), and spicy (the chili)—are my attempt to wipe all those bad memories away and help you make a hot dog that *everyone* will crave. The ultra-crispy, snappy texture of the hot dogs comes from splitting them in half (the long way). If you're thinking of cutting corners, I beg you to not skip the chili (I'll give you a free pass to not make the cheese sauce). Grill the hot dogs outdoors or in a pan on your stovetop.

MAKE THE CHILI: In a large pot, heat the olive oil over medium heat. Add the onion and garlic and sauté until the onion is translucent, 4 to 5 minutes. Add all the chili powder, cumin, cocoa powder, salt, cinnamon, pepper, allspice, cloves, and red pepper flakes and stir to combine. Cook for about 5 minutes, until the spices toast and release their aroma. Pour 2 tablespoons of water into the pot and use a wooden spoon to loosen the cooked spices from the bottom.

Add the meat to the pot and stir to combine. Sauté until the meat is browned through, 5 to 6 minutes.

Add the tomato sauce and vinegar, and stir to combine. Reduce the heat to low, cover, and simmer the chili for about 1½ hours, stirring every 5 to 10 minutes. (If you want to use a slow cooker, pour the mixture into your slow cooker after adding the tomato sauce and vinegar, cover, and cook on high for 3 hours.)

MAKES 6 SERVINGS

For the chili

2 tablespoons olive oil

1½ cups small-diced onion (1 large onion)

2 teaspoons minced garlic

1½ teaspoons chili powder

1 teaspoon ground cumin

1 teaspoon unsweetened cocoa powder

¾ teaspoon salt

½ teaspoon ground cinnamon

¼ teaspoon ground black pepper

¼ teaspoon ground allspice

Pinch of ground cloves

Pinch of red pepper flakes

1 pound ground beef (90–95% lean)

1 (15-ounce) can tomato sauce

1 tablespoon rice vinegar

continued

For the cheese sauce

2 cups milk

8 tablespoons (1 stick) unsalted butter

2 tablespoons all-purpose flour

8 ounces American cheese, cut into cubes, or 12 slices

4 ounces mild cheddar cheese, shredded (½ cup)

½ teaspoon Dijon mustard

½ teaspoon garlic salt

For the hot dogs

6 jumbo all-beef hot dogs

6 King's Hawaiian hot dog buns

1 (24-ounce) container French's crispy fried onions

1 bunch scallions, thinly sliced, for garnish

MAKE THE CHEESE SAUCE: In a small pot, bring the milk to a simmer over medium-high heat. Remove from the heat and set aside.

In a large, high-sided skillet, melt the butter over medium-high heat. Sprinkle the flour over the butter and whisk to combine. Cook until the mixture begins to foam, about 1 minute. While whisking continuously, slowly add the warm milk and whisk until fully incorporated. Bring the mixture to a boil, stirring continuously, and cook for 2 minutes. Turn off the heat and add both cheeses. Whisk until the cheese has melted and the sauce is velvety. Stir in the mustard and garlic salt and keep warm on the back of the stove.

COOK THE HOT DOGS: Heat a grill to high.

Using a sharp knife, split the hot dogs lengthwise three-quarters of the way through. Gently fold the hot dogs open like a book. Lightly score the flesh of the cut sides on an angle in both directions to create a ½-inch crosshatch pattern. Be careful not to cut too deeply and pierce the skin. Place the hot dogs on the hot grill, cut-side down, and close the lid. Cook until the hot dogs begin to char, about 4 minutes, then remove them from the grill.

To serve, place the hot dogs skin-side down in the buns. Spoon a generous amount of chili over each hot dog and ladle 3 to 4 tablespoons of the cheese sauce over the chili. Top with a generous mound of crispy onions and garnish with the scallions. You'll need a fork to eat these—they can get messy!

Notes

★ This chili can be made ahead (and is always better the next day since the spices get a chance to meld overnight), so you can grill and assemble the chili dogs more quickly.

★ Leftover cheese sauce? Mix in a can of drained roasted chiles, and now it's queso dip!

blt4d (blt for dinner)

Prep Time: 5 minutes | Cook Time: 30 minutes

This sandwich is obviously best in the peak of tomato season. But eating an incredible, classic sandwich like this only three months out of the year is a shame, so as long as you can get decent tomatoes, I'll understand if you eat this year-round. This BLT is nothing short of a showstopper. It's like *Hamilton*'s opening night on Broadway, or like finally getting into the theater after waiting in line for the new *Star Wars* movie. Yes, it is *that* good. Maybe it's the fried egg, the seasoned tomato slices, or the melty cheese. . . . A tip for you: Make sure your bacon is not too thin, not too fatty, not too crispy, and not too limp (I'm a bit of a bacon snob). I call this BLT4 dinner . . . it's a hearty, *real* meal with a fried egg as part of the mix, and I promise you won't be looking for a snack an hour later.

Preheat the oven to 400°F.

Arrange the bacon in a single layer on a wire rack set into a rimmed baking sheet. Bake until slightly curled and mostly crisp, 20 to 25 minutes. Pour the bacon fat that has collected on the baking sheet through a strainer and reserve 6 tablespoons.

Lay the tomato slices on a plate in an even layer. Sprinkle the garlic salt evenly over all the slices and set them aside. Remove the outer leaves of the head of lettuce and discard. Cut the core out of the head and set aside the tender inner leaves for the sandwiches.

In a large skillet or griddle, heat 3 tablespoons of the reserved bacon fat over medium heat until melted. Place 4 slices of the bread in the pan, swirling them around to get a good coat of fat on the bottom of each slice. Place 2 cheese slices each on two of the bread slices and let the bread toast in the fat until nicely browned and the cheese is melted, about 6 minutes. Remove the 4 slices of bread from the pan and set aside on your cutting board. Repeat with the remaining bacon fat, bread, and cheddar.

MAKES 4 SERVINGS

16 slices thick-cut bacon

3 medium beefsteak tomatoes, sliced ¼ inch thick

¼ teaspoon garlic salt

1 head Bibb lettuce

8 slices sourdough bread

8 slices sharp cheddar cheese

1 tablespoon vegetable oil

4 eggs

3 tablespoons mayonnaise

2 ripe medium avocados, sliced

continued

While the bread toasts, in a medium skillet, heat the vegetable oil over medium-high heat. Crack the eggs carefully into the pan, being careful not to pop the yolks. Cook, uncovered, until the eggs are mostly cooked, with just a little raw egg white on top, about 3 minutes. Gently flip the eggs and turn the heat off.

Lay the slices of toasted bread on your cutting board. Spread about ¾ tablespoon of the mayo on each plain slice of bread with no cheese. Place an egg on top of the mayo. Lay 4 slices of bacon on top of the egg and top with the salted tomato slices, some avocado, and a couple of lettuce leaves.

Notes

- Since it's virtually impossible to griddle all four sandwiches at once, you'll have to work quickly to make sure the melted cheese stays melted on your first two sandwiches. Try sliding the cheesy bread slices in the turned-off oven (it should still be warm from baking your bacon) while you cook the second round.

- To make the most of your time in the kitchen, cook the eggs while the bread is on the griddle, and prep your lettuce and tomato while the bacon is in the oven.

- If your tomatoes are not quite amazing or if it's not tomato season, try running them under hot tap water for 30 seconds. I find it releases the juices and almost quick-ripens them if they're just a little too firm. Also, use a serrated knife to cut them to avoid smashing.

cornflake-crusted fried chicken sandwiches

Prep Time: 30 minutes | Cook Time: 30 minutes

Let me paint you a picture of this almost-too-good-to-be-true dish. So many things make this recipe amazing. There's the tangy poppy seed coleslaw, the Old Bay mayonnaise (usually affiliated with po'boy sandwiches in Louisiana), and the sweetness from the King's Hawaiian buns that bring harmony to the entire dish. Then there's the chicken—marinated in pickle juice, rolled in cornflakes, then baked until crispy. It is over-the-top incredible . . . so much so that my clients request this recipe in mini-versions for fancy catered events, right next to foie gras and quail!

Preheat the oven to 400°F. Line a baking sheet with parchment paper or aluminum foil and spray generously with cooking spray.

Butterfly the chicken breasts by making a horizontal slice in the thickest part of the breast almost all the way through, then flipping the flap open. Press the breast down slightly with your palm to even it out at the cut. Put the butterflied chicken breasts in a shallow container and toss with the pickle juice, making sure they are all coated. Cover with plastic wrap and marinate at room temperature for 30 minutes or up to 1 hour.

MEANWHILE, MAKE THE SLAW: In a large bowl, whisk together the mayo, vinegar, poppy seeds, sugar, lemon juice, and salt. Add the cabbage and toss to coat. Refrigerate the slaw until the sandwiches are ready to assemble. (You could make the slaw the day before, too.)

MAKE THE MAYO: In a small bowl, whisk together the mayo, lemon juice, and Old Bay. (The seasoned mayo can be prepared the day before, covered, and refrigerated.)

MAKES 4 SERVINGS

Cooking spray

4 small boneless, skinless chicken breasts

4 to 5 extra-sour dill pickles, sliced, plus ¾ cup brine from the jar

For the poppy seed slaw

¾ cup mayonnaise

3 tablespoons apple cider vinegar

3 tablespoons poppy seeds

1 teaspoon sugar

1 teaspoon lemon juice

½ teaspoon salt

1 small-medium head green cabbage, shredded (about 6 cups)

For the Old Bay mayo

½ cup mayonnaise

½ teaspoon lemon juice

½ teaspoon Old Bay seasoning (not the low-sodium or salt-free version)

continued

cornflake-crusted fried chicken sandwiches, continued

To assemble

1 cup all-purpose flour

1 teaspoon garlic salt

4 eggs

4 cups cornflakes

Cooking spray

Kosher salt

4 King's Hawaiian burger buns

COOK THE CHICKEN AND ASSEMBLE THE SANDWICHES: In a large zip-top bag, combine the flour and ½ teaspoon of the garlic salt. Give it a good shake to mix it thoroughly. In a large shallow container (like a glass baking dish) or shallow bowl, whisk the eggs with the remaining ½ teaspoon garlic salt. Pour the cornflakes onto a baking sheet.

Drain the chicken breasts and toss them in the bag with the flour. Seal the bag and shake until the chicken breasts are fully coated. One at a time, dip the floured chicken breasts in the egg mixture, then into the cornflakes. Using your palms, press the chicken down into the cornflakes to make sure you have a really good crunchy coating on both sides. Set the coated chicken breast on the prepared baking sheet and repeat to coat the remaining chicken. Give the coated chicken breasts a light mist of cooking spray on top. Bake the chicken until cooked through and golden brown, about 30 minutes. Immediately transfer the chicken to a wire rack to cool slightly and sprinkle them with a pinch of kosher salt per breast.

To assemble the sandwiches, first spread 1½ tablespoons of the seasoned mayo on each side of the burger buns. (You can toast the buns if you like, but I prefer the soft texture of the untoasted bun against the crisp chicken.) Arrange 5 or 6 slices of pickle on each bottom bun, and top the pickle slices with the chicken breasts. Scoop about ½ cup of the slaw onto each chicken breast and finish the sandwiches with the top bun. Give the sandwiches a gentle press to make sure they don't fall apart while serving.

Notes

★ Be sure to buy regular-size buns, not jumbo ones. There's not much worse than a bun that's too big for the filling!

★ You might have too much slaw for four sandwiches, and that's okay! The slaw is amazing the next day as a side for lunch or on another sandwich (maybe using that frozen roast pork from my hash recipe on page 13? Yum!).

★ I love these sandwiches when the chicken is hot and fresh from the oven, but they are great at room temperature, too. I've also made them as sliders using chicken breast tenders and served them as appetizers, and they are always a showstopper.

★ If you need to marinate the chicken for more than an hour, be sure to refrigerate it. I wouldn't go much longer than an hour, though; the acid in the pickle juice will start to cook the meat, making it a little tough.

★ If you like hot sauce, you have to try Crystal brand hot sauce on this sandwich; it takes it to another level!

cornmeal crust white pizza

Prep Time: 10 minutes | Cook Time: 15 minutes | Inactive time: 1 hour

MAKES ONE 12 X 17-INCH PAN PIZZA

For the crust

1 cup warm water

1 (¼-ounce) packet instant yeast (2¼ teaspoons)

3 tablespoons olive oil, plus 2 to 3 tablespoons for the bowl

1⅔ cups bread flour, plus more for dusting

¼ cup cornmeal, plus 3 to 4 tablespoons for dusting

1½ teaspoons sea salt

⅛ teaspoon sugar

For the pizza

¾ cup heavy cream

2 teaspoons minced garlic

½ teaspoon garlic salt

½ teaspoon onion powder

1 bunch basil, leaves torn into small pieces, stems reserved

4 to 6 tablespoons olive oil

2 cups shredded part-skim mozzarella cheese

1 (4-ounce) ball fresh mozzarella, pulled into shreds

½ cup shredded Parmesan (1½ ounces)

I know, I know. Places like Trader Joe's and Whole Foods sell *really* good and inexpensive pizza crusts. They are great when you have a super-small window of time, and I do use them sometimes. But if you find yourself with even an extra hour to spare, this homemade crust is really worth making. The cornmeal gives this pizza dough a rustic feel and a wonderful crunchy texture. Make no mistake, this is not your Lombardi's New York–style tomato-and-mozzarella pie. My version has a garlicky cream-based sauce with three different kinds of cheese and torn basil. Make this pizza for a family movie night! Maybe watch the '90s *Teenage Mutant Ninja Turtles* movie (good luck describing this live-action, fun-but-cringeworthy staple of our youth to your kids). The Ninja Turtles *love* pizza, so that's the first movie that comes to mind for me. Even if they don't quite get the movie, at least the pizza will be a hit!

MAKE THE CRUST: In a medium bowl, combine the warm water and yeast. Add 3 tablespoons of the olive oil, the flour, cornmeal, salt, and sugar. Stir with a wooden spoon until the dough resembles a shaggy mass and is completely hydrated. If the dough looks a little dry, add a little more water by the tablespoon. It should be tacky and moist but not super-sticky.

Grease a large bowl with 2 to 3 tablespoons olive oil. Turn the dough out onto a floured work surface. Knead by hand for about 7 minutes (or in a stand mixer fitted with the dough hook for 5 minutes). Round the kneaded dough into a ball and put it in the oiled bowl. Cover with plastic wrap and set aside in a warm place to rise until doubled in size, about 1 hour.

WHILE THE DOUGH RISES, MAKE THE CREAM SAUCE: In a small pot, combine the cream, garlic, garlic salt, and onion powder. Bring to a simmer over medium-low heat. Reduce the heat to low and simmer until slightly thickened, 3 to 4 minutes. Turn the heat off, add the basil stems, and set aside to cool.

continued

2 lemon wedges

Large pinch of Maldon sea salt

Large pinch of red pepper flakes

Preheat the oven to 450°F. Pour 3 to 4 tablespoons of olive oil onto a 12 x 17-inch baking sheet and use a pastry brush or paper towel to spread it evenly over the bottom and sides of the pan. Sprinkle 3 to 4 tablespoons of cornmeal evenly over the oiled pan.

Once the dough has risen, turn it out onto your floured work surface. Gently push and roll the dough out with your hands into a rough rectangle shape almost the size of your baking sheet. Transfer the dough rectangle to the prepared pan and push it into the corners, stretching the dough as evenly as you can. If the dough is sticky, pour 1 to 2 tablespoons olive oil on your hands before handling it.

Once the dough is stretched to fill the baking sheet, pull the basil stems out of the cream sauce (discard them) and drizzle the sauce over the surface of the dough, trying not to get any sauce on the outer inch of the dough (the edge of the crust). Use the back of a large spoon or a pastry brush to spread the sauce evenly over the pizza. Sprinkle the shredded mozzarella over the pizza, and top that with the pulled fresh mozzarella. Add the shredded Parmesan evenly over the top of the pizza. Bake until the crust is well browned and the cheese is bubbling and starting to brown in a few spots, 12 to 15 minutes. Take the pizza out of the oven and immediately sprinkle the torn basil leaves over the hot cheese and drizzle with 2 tablespoons olive oil. Squeeze the lemon wedges over the pizza and sprinkle with the Maldon salt and red pepper flakes just before serving.

Notes

⋆ I love a good simple white pizza, but feel free to add additional toppings to your taste. Fresh baby spinach would be awesome (added on top of the sauce and under the cheeses to prevent burning), and halved cherry tomatoes would also be great (add them on top of the cheese).

⋆ This amount of dough will make one thin- to regular-crust rectangular pizza or two thin-crust round pizzas. If rolling and stretching the dough to fit a baking sheet is too hard, divide the dough in half and roll each piece into a 12-inch round. If you like a fluffy thick crust, double the recipe and fit the dough into the baking sheet.

lesley's corned beef and braised cabbage

Prep Time: 10 minutes | Cook Time: 2½ hours

Lesley is the one who makes this dish in our home, not me. I just stand by with a fork while she works her magic, ready to chow down once it is done. She gave me this recipe so I could include it in the book. My only true contribution is the addition of the braised cabbage on the side, which takes Lesley's recipe over the top (and goes great on corned beef hash with poached eggs the next day). If you ask her, she prefers to throw the cabbage in *with* the corned beef while it simmers, but either way, you can't go wrong. I recommend that you enjoy this dish not just on St. Paddy's Day. It deserves a *lot* more playtime than that! A chef's tip for you: Keep in mind that although the ingredients are simple, it all comes down to a really good cut of meat. It's worth the extra dollar for the best end result.

MAKE THE CORNED BEEF: Put the corned beef brisket (and any included spices) in a large stockpot. Pour the beer over the brisket and then pour in enough cold water to completely cover the meat. Add the sliced onions, bay leaves, and garlic cloves and bring to a boil over high heat. Skim any foam that floats to the top. Cover, reduce the heat to low, and simmer the corned beef until tender, about 2½ hours.

WHILE THE MEAT COOKS, MAKE THE BRAISED CABBAGE: Cut the cabbage in half lengthwise and remove the core. Cut each half into 6 slices.

In a large sauté pan, heat 2 tablespoons of the olive oil over medium-high heat. Add the cabbage and break it up with a wooden spoon. Press the cabbage against the pan and cook, undisturbed, to get a good dark sear, about 15 minutes. Stir the browned bits into the cabbage and make a well in the center, exposing the bottom of the pan. Pour the remaining 1 tablespoon olive oil into the well and add the cumin, caraway, and red pepper flakes. Stir the spices continuously while toasting (still just in the very center of the pan) until they become fragrant and start

MAKES 6 TO 8 SERVINGS

For the corned beef

1 (3- to 3½-pound) corned beef brisket (with corning spices included)

1 (12-ounce) can light beer, such as Coors Light

5 to 6 cups cold water

2 large yellow onions, cut into ½-inch-thick rings

3 bay leaves

3 garlic cloves, peeled

For the braised cabbage

1 medium-large head cabbage

3 tablespoons olive oil

1 teaspoon cumin seeds

1 teaspoon caraway seeds

¼ teaspoon red pepper flakes

1 medium apple, cored and diced (about 1 cup)

1 medium onion, diced (about 1½ cups)

1 tablespoon minced garlic

1 large jalapeño, seeded and minced (about ¼ cup)

2 teaspoons garlic salt

½ teaspoon kosher salt

continued

lesley's corned beef and braised cabbage, continued

sizzling and popping, about 1 minute. Add the apple, onion, garlic, jalapeño, garlic salt, salt, and black pepper and stir everything in the pan together. Raise the heat to high and cook, stirring frequently, until the cabbage is completely wilted and the apple and onion are translucent, about 5 minutes. Stir in the mustard, vinegar, and broth and reduce the heat to low. Cover and simmer the cabbage until it has absorbed most of the liquid, 6 to 7 minutes. Turn the heat off, add the cold butter and lemon juice, and stir to combine. Gently fold in the parsley.

When the corned beef has finished cooking, turn off the heat and let the meat rest for at least 15 minutes before slicing. Serve the corned beef with the cooked onions and braised cabbage.

Notes

✶ Be sure to let the meat rest before slicing. Also, always slice against the grain!

✶ To make sure the butter emulsifies properly into the cabbage, add it in two chunks and make sure it is cold. That way, it will melt slowly into the mixture and incorporate into the sauce instead of creating an oil slick on top.

¼ teaspoon ground black pepper

1 tablespoon whole-grain mustard

1 tablespoon apple cider vinegar

2 cups chicken broth

3 tablespoons cold unsalted butter

1 tablespoon lemon juice

1 bunch flat-leaf parsley, coarsely chopped (about 1 cup loosely packed)

butternut and brussels shepherd's pie

Prep Time: 30 minutes | Cook Time: 45 minutes

MAKES 6 SERVINGS

2 small or 1 large butternut squash

6 tablespoons olive oil

2 teaspoons kosher salt

1 pound ground turkey (80% to 90% lean)

2 cups small-diced onions (about 2 medium)

1½ cups diced mushrooms (4 ounces)

2 cups small-diced carrots (3 to 4 medium)

1 cup small-diced celery (3 to 4 stalks)

1 teaspoon minced garlic

½ teaspoon ground black pepper

½ teaspoon dried thyme

2¾ cups chicken broth

3 tablespoons cornstarch

4 tablespoons (½ stick) unsalted butter, melted

¼ cup milk

2 cups thinly sliced Brussels sprouts (7 ounces)

2 scallions, thinly sliced

1 cup shredded Parmesan cheese (4 ounces)

For me, this dish screams fall/winter, but I promise that the lightness of lean turkey and the caramelized Brussels sprouts make it awesome any time of year. I love making this when my in-laws are coming over to our house. I prep it ahead, freeze it, and then pop it in the oven when they walk through the door—in no time, dinner is ready and I look like a super-organized/time-efficient cook. Win-win! One thing I've learned when it comes to cooking for my family is that it is all about working ahead. Freezing meals and eating *yesterday's* dish *today* while cooking *today* for *tomorrow* allows for flexibility in my schedule and often covers my a** when I'm short on time or traveling. This is like a cheap insurance policy for the craziness of life.

Preheat the oven to 400°F. Line a baking sheet with parchment paper or aluminum foil.

Cut the butternut squash in half lengthwise and scoop out the seeds. Drizzle the cut halves with 3 tablespoons of the olive oil and sprinkle with ½ teaspoon of the salt. Place the squash cut-side down on the prepared baking sheet. Bake for 30 minutes, until the squash is cooked soft and the bottoms start to caramelize. Insert a paring knife into the squash skin to test; if there is no resistance, the squash is done. Set the cooked squash aside to cool while you make the shepherd's pie filling.

In a large sauté pan, heat 2 tablespoons olive oil over medium-high heat. Add the turkey and cook, stirring continuously, until browned, 4 to 5 minutes. Add the onion, mushrooms, carrot, celery, minced garlic, 1 teaspoon salt, the pepper, and thyme. Continue sautéing, stirring frequently, until the onions become translucent and the carrots soften, 5 to 6 minutes.

continued

butternut and brussels shepherd's pie, continued

Add 2½ cups of the chicken broth to the sauté pan, and stir to combine. Lower the heat to medium-low. In a small bowl, mix the cornstarch and the remaining ¼ cup chicken broth until smooth. Pour the cornstarch slurry into the turkey filling, stirring continuously. Once all the slurry is in and completely mixed, increase the heat to high and cook for 1 minute, stirring continuously, until the mixture has thickened. Turn the heat off and pour the turkey mixture into a 9 x 13-inch baking dish or casserole.

Once they are cool enough to handle, scoop the butternut squash from the skins into a medium bowl. Add the melted butter, milk, and ¼ teaspoon salt. Mash with a potato masher or an electric mixer until smooth.

In a medium bowl, toss the Brussels sprouts, scallions, remaining 1 tablespoon olive oil, and remaining ¼ teaspoon salt. Sprinkle the Brussels sprout mixture over the turkey in the baking dish, making an even layer.

Increase the oven temperature to 450°F.

Scoop the butternut squash puree evenly on top of the Brussels sprout layer and spread it evenly. Sprinkle the Parmesan cheese over the entire casserole and bake until the filling bubbles, about 10 minutes. Switch the oven to broil and put the casserole under the broiler on the highest rack to brown the cheese, 4 to 5 minutes. Let the casserole sit for 5 minutes before serving.

Notes

- Feel free to play with the veggies in the turkey gravy; I like to add whatever I've got in the fridge or freezer. Frozen peas, green beans, and spinach would all be delicious.

- If prepping ahead and freezing, wrap the whole baking dish tightly in plastic wrap and store it flat in the freezer. When it's time to cook, unwrap the casserole and bake it at 350°F for 30 to 40 minutes, until bubbling and hot throughout. Then pop it under the broiler to brown the cheese.

one-pot turkey "scott family helper"

Prep Time: 5 minutes | Cook Time: 30 minutes

I mentioned this in my last cookbook, but I call my mom the "David Copperfield of ground beef." She can start with ground beef and then POOF! A vast array of dishes appears! Like many families in the 1970s and '80s, our family had Hamburger Helper on hand for times when a quick and inexpensive meal was needed (and also just because it was one of my favorites). Even though it is 2020, that does not mean that Olive can't experience some favorite flavors from my childhood; this is just a "2.0 version" made with lean ground turkey. Although I don't sneak veggies like kale, spinach, or zucchini into this recipe, it can be done quite easily. Oh, and *never* skimp on the cheddar cheese. I wouldn't be able to call it "Scott Family Helper" with a measly amount of cheese! Switch out the meat, if you like, and if you are gluten-free, you can switch out the pasta for a gluten-free variety, too.

In a large casserole, heat the olive oil over medium-high heat. Add the turkey and cook, stirring, about 5 minutes until half of the meat is still pink. Add the onion, garlic, and tomato and sauté until the garlic is fragrant, about 1 minute. Add the ketchup, parsley, garlic powder, ground mustard, Dijon mustard, paprika, salt, pepper, and nutmeg and stir to combine. Cook, stirring frequently, until the spices are fragrant and the liquid has almost completely evaporated, 3 to 4 minutes. Turn off the heat and add the pasta and broth. Stir to combine and scrape up any browned bits from the sides and bottom of the pot with a wooden spoon (that's the flavor right there!). Bring the mixture up to a simmer over high heat, then reduce the heat to medium-low and simmer, uncovered, until the pasta is al dente, about 6 minutes. Turn the heat off and add the cheddar, sour cream, and hot sauce. Stir until the cheese has melted and the sauce is completely creamy. Let the pasta sit for at least 15 minutes so the sauce can thicken. Sprinkle the parsley over the top, then serve.

MAKES 4 TO 6 SERVINGS

2 tablespoons olive oil

1 pound ground turkey (80% to 90% lean)

½ large yellow onion, grated (about ½ cup)

1 tablespoon minced garlic

1 medium tomato, grated or crushed (½ cup)

2 tablespoons ketchup

1 tablespoon dried parsley

2 teaspoons garlic powder

2 teaspoons yellow mustard powder

1 teaspoon Dijon mustard

1 teaspoon smoked paprika

½ teaspoon salt

½ teaspoon ground black pepper

¼ teaspoon ground nutmeg

1½ cups dried elbow pasta

3 cups chicken broth

2 cups shredded cheddar cheese (8 ounces)

½ cup sour cream

½ teaspoon hot sauce (I like Crystal for this recipe)

½ cup coarsely chopped fresh parsley

continued

Notes

⭐ The macaroni will continue to cook and soften after you turn off the heat, so be careful to cook it just to al dente. Overcooking the pasta will result in a mushy dish (Lesley is big on texture so I definitely can't make that mistake!).

⭐ To make this a complete meal, add a bag of frozen veggies just when the macaroni is al dente. (Broccoli florets, peas, spinach, and carrots would all work great here.) Bring the mixture back up a simmer, then turn off the heat and add the cheese and sour cream.

⭐ Not all hot sauces are created equal. Each brand uses a different ratio of vinegar and spice, and some add sweetness as well. Play with different brands and amounts for this recipe and see what you like best! Just remember that you can always add more, but you can't take it out.

⭐ If you want this dish to be beefy, by all means, substitute ground beef. Try to stick to at least 90% lean ground beef to avoid the extra fat.

veggies and sides

the go-to grain grid

This grid is a great reference that will take you one step further than just following the cooking instructions on the back of a bag of rice. Layering flavors is important, so by using bouillon and garlic when cooking the grains, a really flavorful base is created. If you shop in bulk like I do, you may not even have a bag with the cooking instructions on the back, so by having this grid as a visual reference, the liquid-to-grain ratio will never be a mystery.

MAKES 2 CUPS COOKED GRAINS

1 cup grain

1½ to 2½ cups water (see grid)

1½ teaspoons Better Than Bouillon vegetable base

1 teaspoon minced garlic

2 bay leaves

GRAIN, UNCOOKED	WATER (PER 1 CUP GRAIN)	COOKING TIME, STOVETOP	COOKING TIME, RICE COOKER	GRAIN PREP
brown rice	2½ cups	45 minutes	45 to 50 minutes	rinse in strainer
white rice	1½ cups	20 minutes	20 to 25 minutes	rinse 3 times, until water runs clear
quinoa	1½ cups	20 minutes	20 to 25 minutes	rinse in strainer

Rinse the grain.

If using a rice cooker, combine the grain, water, bouillon paste, garlic, and bay leaves in the cooking insert. Whisk the ingredients together until the bouillon paste has dissolved. Put the lid on and set the rice cooker according to the manufacturer's directions. When the grain is done cooking, remove the lid and let stand to cool and stop the cooking.

If cooking on the stovetop, in a small pot, whisk the ingredients together until the bouillon paste has dissolved. Bring the mixture to a boil, then immediately reduce the heat to low. Cover the pot with a tight-fitting lid and simmer for the time specified in the grain grid. Remove from the heat and uncover the pot, but do not stir the grains yet! Let the steam dissipate and allow the grains to cool in the pot for at least 15 minutes before stirring to avoid gummy, overcooked grains.

crispy brussels sprouts with parmesan dressing

Prep Time: 5 minutes | Cook Time: 20 minutes

Once upon a time at one of my first restaurants, I created this awesome side dish, which before long became my most popular veggie side! Take your halved Brussels sprouts and blister them until they are almost too dark, then, while they are hot, toss them in the Parmesan dressing so they suck up all the flavorful goodness like delicious little sponges as they cool. I like adding some form of chile, such as Calabrian chile or sambal, an Indonesian chile sauce that is easy to find at the grocery store. Spiced up or not, these Brussels sprouts are incredible. This would be a fun Thanksgiving side dish (something different than the usual green bean casserole) or tossed over mixed greens for a fresh and fabulous lunch.

Preheat the oven to 425°F. Place a large rimmed baking sheet in the oven to preheat.

MAKE THE DRESSING: In a food processor or blender, combine the Parmesan, yogurt, garlic, olive oil, lemon juice, pepper, and Worcestershire and puree until smooth. Transfer to a bowl and stir in the basil. Set aside.

MAKE THE BRUSSELS SPROUTS: In a large bowl, toss the Brussels sprouts, olive oil, salt, and pepper.

MAKES 4 SERVINGS

For the Parmesan dressing

⅔ cup grated Parmesan cheese

½ cup plain full-fat Greek yogurt

1 garlic clove

2 tablespoons extra-virgin olive oil

1 tablespoon lemon juice

½ teaspoon freshly ground black pepper

¼ teaspoon Worcestershire sauce

¼ cup packed fresh basil leaves, chopped

For the Brussels sprouts

1 pound Brussels sprouts, trimmed and halved

3 tablespoons extra-virgin olive oil

1 teaspoon kosher salt

½ teaspoon freshly ground black pepper

continued

Carefully remove the hot baking sheet from the oven. Dump the Brussels sprouts onto the baking sheet and shake the pan to evenly distribute them. Roast, undisturbed, until deep dark brown around the edges, about 20 minutes.

Immediately toss the hot Brussels sprouts with ½ cup of the dressing and transfer to a serving dish. Add more dressing to your taste and serve.

Note

★ This recipe makes more dressing than you might need for 1 pound of Brussel sprouts. Store the dressing in an airtight container in the refrigerator for up to 1 week and use it on other roasted veggies or as a dip for fresh crudités.

slow-baked 3/2/1 spaghetti squash

Prep Time: 5 minutes | Cook Time: 120 minutes | Inactive Time: 40 minutes (cooling)

MAKES 4 SERVINGS

1 (3½-pound) spaghetti squash

1 tablespoon extra-virgin olive oil

¼ cup plus 2 teaspoons 3/2/1 Lemon-Soy Vinaigrette (page 63)

6 scallions, thinly sliced (1 packed cup)

2 tablespoons toasted sesame seeds

Notes

★ Line the baking sheet with aluminum foil for a fuss-free cleanup.

★ Just like pasta, I like my spaghetti squash to be al dente.

I am not afraid of making fun of myself, and this dish comes with a great (and embarrassing) story. Back in 1999, when I was in culinary school, I had the rookie idea to use spaghetti squash in a soup . . . pureed. I remember my instructor saying, "Out of all of the squash that you could have picked, you used *this* squash for soup?" In that embarrassing moment, I realized I had really messed up. But I learned a life lesson: If the name of a food literally *tells* you how to use it, do what it says! Since then, I have come up with so many ways to use spaghetti squash, and it has never failed me. Of all my vegetable dishes, this is Lesley's favorite. When it comes to roasting the squash, please note that it cannot be rushed. Be sure to cook it for the time I've indicated, and enjoy its willingness to become anything you want it to be!

Preheat the oven to 300°F. Line a baking sheet with aluminum foil.

Using a chef's knife, carefully make six slits, each about ¼ inch deep, around the squash. Trim off a ¼-inch-thick slice from one side of the squash to make a flat surface (this will prevent it from rolling around on the pan). Place the squash on the prepared baking sheet and bake for 2 hours, or until the squash gives easily when pierced with a paring knife. Let the squash cool on the baking sheet for 30 minutes.

Halve the squash lengthwise and, using a spoon, remove and discard the seeds, then let the squash to cool for 10 minutes more.

Using a fork, go around the rim of the squash to loosen the flesh from the skin. Pull the flesh toward the center to gently separate it into spaghetti-like strands.

Drizzle the squash with the dressing, dividing it evenly between the two halves. Top with the scallions and toasted sesame seeds and serve.

roasted scallions
with tomato-almond relish

Prep Time: 10 minutes | Cook Time: 6 minutes

This side dish was a huge seller at my restaurant Mason. In Spain, young leeks or scallions are put on hot embers to char them. The outside layers are then peeled off and the tender, inner portion is dipped in sauce to enjoy. It is so delectable! I love taking inspiration from other country's cuisines, and this is my simpler "Scott house" version, born of that Spanish dish. I feel like Dr. Seuss saying this, but I love scallions in a pot, when they're hot, any day, and in every way! They're inexpensive and super-delicious, and they love being charred on the grill (I know, because I talk to my food). Take the room-temperature tomato-almond relish and spoon it over the hot scallions for a mind-blowing taste experience. I joke that this dish could convert any meat eater to a vegetarian (at least for a few hours). But I also love spooning this delectable relish over fish, chicken, or even pork chops. I sure do *relish* my relishes!

Preheat the oven to 500°F. Line a baking sheet with aluminum foil (do not use parchment paper—it will burn) and place it in the oven to preheat for at least 5 minutes.

MAKE THE RELISH: In a medium bowl, combine the garlic, jalapeño, salt, pepper, vinegar, lemon juice, and olive oil. Let sit for 5 minutes. Dice the tomatoes into small pieces; you should have about 1 cup. Add the tomatoes, parsley, and almonds to the bowl and stir gently to combine without bruising the parsley or breaking up the tomatoes. Set aside.

MAKE THE SCALLIONS: Cut the root ends and top ½ inch off the scallions. Peel off any brown or slimy layers from the white ends. In a large bowl, toss the scallions with the olive oil, salt, and pepper.

MAKES 4 SERVINGS

For the relish

1 teaspoon minced garlic

½ large jalapeño, seeded and minced (about 2 tablespoons)

¼ teaspoon salt

¼ teaspoon ground black pepper

1 teaspoon white wine vinegar

1½ teaspoons lemon juice

2 tablespoons olive oil

2 medium tomatoes

2 tablespoons coarsely chopped fresh flat-leaf parsley

¼ cup coarsely chopped dry-roasted unsalted almonds

For the scallions

3 bunches scallions

3 tablespoons olive oil

½ teaspoon kosher salt

¼ teaspoon ground black pepper

continued

roasted scallions with tomato-almond relish, continued

Very carefully take the hot baking sheet from the oven and pour the scallions onto it. Give the pan a quick shake to settle them in a single layer and put it back in the oven on the highest rack. Roast the scallions until the greens are very dark and burnt at the edges and the whites are starting to brown, about 6 minutes.

Transfer the scallions to a serving dish and pour the relish over the top. Serve immediately, or let cool and serve at room temperature. Served right away, the scallion greens will have a crisp texture; later on, they will soften after they have had a chance to soak up the relish. Either way, this dish is a winner.

Notes

* Trust me, you want these scallions burnt. The taste is sweet, complex, and just amazing.

* Just like with my pico de gallo (see page 135), I like to macerate the jalapeño and garlic with lemon juice before adding the tomatoes. This step really helps to break down the spice and mellow everything out. If you want it spicy, keep some (or all) of the jalapeño seeds in the mix.

the "perfect" asparagus with pistachio pistou

Prep Time: 5 minutes | Cook Time: 5 minutes

Let me clear up a common misconception: Asparagus is *not* just a spring vegetable. Long gone are those days—you'll find it at most grocery stores during all four seasons. Also gone are the days of overcooking this vegetable by boiling the heck out of it in salted water until it resembles a limp piece of pasta. My tip for cooking asparagus to perfection is also the same technique that I use with potatoes, Brussels sprouts, scallions, tomatoes, and so much more: Place the asparagus on a blistering-hot baking sheet just pulled from the oven, then pop it back in to roast! This helps to cook the asparagus from the bottom *and* the top—a kind of double cooking that results in the most amazing caramelization and cuts the cooking time in half. Pour the pistachio pistou over the top of the warm asparagus and enjoy this dish year-round.

Preheat the oven to 500°F. Line a baking sheet with aluminum foil (do not use parchment paper—it will burn) and place it in the oven to preheat for at least 5 minutes. You want it screamin' hot!

In a large bowl, toss the asparagus with the olive oil, salt, and pepper. Quickly (and carefully) take the hot pan from the oven and toss the oiled asparagus onto it. Spread the asparagus out evenly in a single layer (I do this by shaking the pan) and return the pan to the oven. Roast for 4 to 5 minutes, until the asparagus are cooked al dente and browning at the tops.

MEANWHILE, MAKE THE PISTOU: In a food processor or blender, combine the pistachios, basil, parsley, garlic, lemon zest and juice, olive oil, and salt. Pulse until coarsely chopped and mixed well.

Serve the asparagus, piping hot or at room temp, topped with the pistou.

MAKES 4 SERVINGS

For the asparagus

2 bunches asparagus, white/purple ends snapped off

3 tablespoons olive oil

1 teaspoon salt

¼ teaspoon ground black pepper

For the pistou

1 cup unsalted shelled pistachios

1 cup loosely packed fresh basil leaves

1 cup loosely packed fresh parsley

1 garlic clove

Zest and juice of 1 lemon

⅔ cup olive oil

¼ teaspoon salt

continued

the "perfect" asparagus with pistachio pistou, continued

Notes

* Snap off the bottom of your asparagus by hand; the asparagus will naturally break where the tough bottom ends meet the yummy tender portion.

* Try walnuts instead of pistachios in the pistou for a nuttier flavor, or go traditional with pine nuts. If you have allergies, omit the nuts altogether and add a little Parmesan cheese.

* If you don't have a food processor, chop the nuts and herbs by hand and stir it all together in a bowl for a rustic, chunky sauce.

* I don't have a lot of time, and I love to make healthy delicious food for my family. I can make a big batch of pistou and keep it in the fridge or freezer, then cook up a quick batch of any seasonal veggie (asparagus is one of my faves) in 5 minutes using my quick-roasting method and top it with the pistou. When it's this easy and delicious, there's no excuse to not eat my veggies!

* Be sure to buy jumbo or large asparagus for this recipe, if possible; the hard-roasting technique will dry out and ruin pencil-thin asparagus (save those petite guys for salad or a quick blanching in salted water).

curried cauliflower with cranberries, cilantro, and almonds

Prep Time: 10 to 15 minutes | Cook Time: 10 minutes

MAKES 4 SERVINGS

1 (2-pound) bag cauliflower florets, or 2 small heads cauliflower, cut into bite-size florets

¼ cup plus 2 tablespoons olive oil

¾ teaspoon salt

1 teaspoon curry powder

1 tablespoon white wine vinegar

½ cup dried cranberries

½ bunch cilantro, chopped (about ½ cup)

½ cup dry-roasted almonds, coarsely chopped

Curry and cauliflower go together like the sportscasters Kruk and Kuip (for my San Francisco peeps); like Chip and Joanna (for my HGTV peeps) and like RuPaul and stilettos (for my San Francisco Castro fam)! Here's another recipe that uses the same "sheet pan method" I use for Brussels sprouts (see page 177) and asparagus (see page 185). Cauliflower is inexpensive and easy to find, and it's a true vegetable chameleon that loves to be transformed. It also comes in a variety of interesting colors. I've found that the more color it acquires in the cooking process, the deeper and richer its flavor profile becomes. When dried cranberries, almonds, and cilantro join cauliflower's ranks, it becomes one of my all-time favorite combos. Bring this dish to a potluck or picnic, and you'll be the most popular guest. Remember to add the dressing while the cauliflower is hot and most willing to soak up all the flavors!

Preheat the oven to 500°F. Line a baking sheet with aluminum foil (do not use parchment paper—it will burn) and place it in the oven to preheat for at least 5 minutes.

In a large bowl, toss the cauliflower florets with ¼ cup of the olive oil and ½ teaspoon of the salt. Very carefully remove the hot baking sheet from the oven. Quickly pour the cauliflower onto the hot pan and give it a shake to spread the florets in an even layer. Return the pan to the oven and roast for 8 to 10 minutes, until the smaller pieces of cauliflower look very dark, almost burnt, and the rest are a medium brown.

While the cauliflower cooks, in a small saucepan, heat the remaining 2 tablespoons olive oil over low heat for 2 to 3 minutes, just until hot. Remove from the heat and whisk in the curry powder, then add the remaining ¼ teaspoon salt and the vinegar and whisk to combine. Set aside.

In a small microwaveable bowl, combine the cranberries and 2 tablespoons of water. Cover tightly with plastic wrap and microwave on high for 30 to 45 seconds, until the water is hot and beginning to soak into the cranberries.

When the cauliflower is done, immediately pour the curry vinaigrette over it and gently fold to coat the cauliflower. Transfer the contents of the pan to a bowl, add the soaked cranberries and cilantro, and toss to combine. Top with the chopped almonds. Serve hot or at room temperature.

Notes

- If your oven won't go to 500°F, use your broiler and adjust the rack so that the food is at least 3 inches from the heat source.

- There are few things tastier than deeply caramelized cauliflower. It may look burnt, but the best parts are the salty, dark brown bits at the edge of the pan. It almost tastes like popcorn!

- If you can, use Madras curry powder. The flavor is so much better than regular curry powder, sweeter and more complex.

oven-roasted broccoli with 3/2/1 lemon-soy vinaigrette

Prep Time: 5 minutes | Cook Time: 6 minutes

You may have realized that my 3/2/1 Lemon-Soy Vinaigrette is one of the "main characters" in this book. It has a permanent place in my fridge, right next to ketchup and mustard. I love to pair it with broccoli in this recipe because it is a super-versatile vegetable that people often overlook. Many people cut off the stems but I like to use the *whole* stalk and of course the tops, cutting them into sixths or eighths for ease in preparation. By using every bit of the broccoli, you are getting *all* of the nutrition that this vegetable has to offer *and* stretching your dollar! When the caramelized pieces of broccoli, with their delicate crunch, hit the lemon-soy vinaigrette . . . all I can say is "mic drop."

Preheat the oven to 500°F. Line a baking sheet with aluminum foil (do not use parchment paper—it will burn) and place it in the oven to preheat for at least 5 minutes.

In a jar or small container, combine 2 tablespoons of the olive oil, the lemon juice, soy sauce, and garlic salt, cover, and shake to mix thoroughly and dissolve the salt. Set aside.

MAKES 4 SERVINGS

4 tablespoons olive oil

2 tablespoons lemon juice

1 tablespoon soy sauce

½ teaspoon garlic salt

1 large head broccoli

continued

Cut the bottom inch off the broccoli stem and cut the head into long strips. Put the broccoli in a large bowl and toss with the remaining 2 tablespoons olive oil. Very carefully take the hot baking sheet from the oven and pour the broccoli onto it. Give the pan a quick shake to settle the broccoli into an even layer and put the pan back in the oven on the highest rack. Roast the broccoli until it is very dark (just about burnt) at the edges of the florets and starting to get tender, about 6 minutes. Take the pan out of the oven and pour the vinaigrette over the broccoli. Be careful of the steam! Use tongs to toss the broccoli in the dressing to fully coat. The florets should soak up all that flavor. Let the broccoli cool a little on the pan, then transfer it to a serving bowl and serve.

Notes

- This recipe uses my 3/2/1 ratio for oil, lemon juice, and soy sauce, but I've taken half the oil and used it to toss the broccoli before cooking.

- You won't believe it until you try it, but broccoli is tastiest when it is almost burnt. Those crispy blackened bits are somehow the sweetest and most flavorful.

- Let the broccoli cool a little on the pan before transferring it to a serving bowl to prevent overcooking. There's not much worse than mushy, overcooked broccoli.

miso-glazed stuffed zucchini with quinoa, kale, and edamame

Prep Time: 10 minutes | Cook Time: 15 minutes

This is the recipe that comes to mind when I realize that swimsuit season is just around the corner! Every time I've served this, I've been faced with the sad truth that I haven't made enough. So trust me, make *two* halves for every *one* person you're feeding because these will go like hotcakes. This is my new, cooler version of all of those recipes from the '80s that used (and sometimes abused) zucchini. I wanted to redeem this incredible squash after years of it being adulterated by eager chefs who were trying to incorporate veggies into their dishes but didn't really want consumers to *know* they were eating veggies. Remember when it was popular to deep-fry zucchini beyond recognition or cover it in Parmesan so completely that it was basically a Parmesan dish with a side of zucchini? Such a shame—zucchini has so much more to offer! Whether served up hot or at room temp, this recipe is a winner. Feel free to switch out the kale for arugula or spinach, if you prefer.

Preheat the oven to broil (or to 500°F).

Cut the zucchini in half lengthwise and scoop out the flesh with a small spoon. Be sure to leave a good amount of zucchini flesh on the sides to hold the filling, ⅛ to ¼ inch.

MAKE THE DRESSING: In a blender, combine the vegetable oil, 2 tablespoons of water, vinegar, mustard, lemon juice, agave, miso, sesame oil, sriracha, and salt. Blend until creamy and well mixed, about 1 minute.

MAKES 6 ZUCCHINI BOATS

3 medium/large zucchini

For the dressing
½ cup vegetable oil

2 tablespoons white wine vinegar

1 tablespoon Dijon mustard

1 tablespoon lemon juice

1 tablespoon agave syrup

1 tablespoon white miso paste

¾ teaspoon toasted sesame oil

½ teaspoon sriracha

¼ teaspoon kosher salt

¾ teaspoon kosher salt

½ teaspoon ground black pepper

½ bunch Lacinato (dinosaur or Tuscan) kale

½ cup frozen shelled edamame beans, thawed and drained

¾ cup cooked quinoa (see grain grid, page 176)

1 teaspoon lemon juice

continued

Brush 3 to 4 tablespoons of the miso dressing on the insides of the zucchini boats. Sprinkle the boats with ¼ teaspoon of salt and ¼ teaspoon of pepper, and broil on the highest rack until the edges start to brown and caramelize, about 15 minutes.

While the zucchini broils, de-stem and cut the kale into thin ribbons. Run your knife through the kale once more to get a nice small rough chop.

In a large bowl, combine the kale, edamame, quinoa, the remaining ½ teaspoon salt, remaining ¼ teaspoon pepper, the lemon juice, and 3 tablespoons of the dressing. Toss well to coat everything with the dressing.

Brush the broiled zucchini boats with another 2 to 3 tablespoons of the miso dressing. Fill the boats with the quinoa mixture, mounding it high. Drizzle a little more dressing over the tops of the stuffed zucchinis with a teaspoon and serve. These are perfect at room temperature as a complete lunch, or as a side for fish or chicken.

Notes

* These boats store really well; try packing them for your lunch or making them ahead for meal prepping.

* When making the dressing, be sure to add the liquids to the blender before the miso to prevent the paste from getting stuck under the blender blades.

* If your zucchini are really large, you may have to double the amount of filling. Try to stick to medium zucchini for this recipe.

lemon-and-parmesan-crusted grilled artichokes

Prep Time: 5 minutes | Cook Time: 30 minutes

Even as a chef, I do *not* have an equal amount of patience for each food that I prepare. Am I the only person who thinks artichokes are a bit hard to deal with? (This is not a rhetorical question—I'm seriously asking!) Anyhow, that just means that when you *do* prepare them, the finished dish should be so incredible, it's worth the trouble. Meyer lemons grow in a lot of our neighbors' yards, and we are lucky enough to reap some of the benefits of their overstock. Artichoke and lemon are a fabulous combination, and I think that 'chokes always call for cheese. I love to grill them after poaching because I'm a big fan of the contrast in texture that grilling provides. The crunchy bits are my favorite. If you like, you can skip the grilling and the Parmesan butter and simply dip the poached artichokes in mayo. But I encourage you to take that extra step. I may have regretted some things (aka hairstyles) over the years, but never once have I regretted grilling a 'choke!

Wash the artichokes under cold running tap water. Using a heavy knife, cut ¼ inch off the bottom of the stems. Pull off the lower petals that are small and tough. Using a peeler, take the skin off the stems. Cut off the top inch of the artichokes, then cut each in half lengthwise.

Rub the cut side of one of the lemon halves over the artichoke halves so they won't discolor. (Alternatively, you can put the cut artichokes in a bowl of cold water with lemon juice.)

In a heavy-bottomed pot, combine the broth, 4 cups of water, wine, the remaining halved lemons, the parsley, garlic, bay leaves, half the lemon zest, 3 tablespoons of the salt, and the peppercorns. Bring the poaching liquid to a boil, then add the artichokes and reduce the heat to maintain a simmer. Place a saucer on top

continued

MAKES 4 TO 6 SERVINGS

4 whole artichokes

4 lemons, zested and halved

4 cups chicken broth

1 cup white wine

½ bunch parsley

8 garlic cloves, smashed and peeled

2 bay leaves

3 tablespoons plus 1 teaspoon kosher salt

1 tablespoon whole black peppercorns

8 tablespoons (1 stick) unsalted butter, at room temperature

1 cup grated Parmesan cheese

1 teaspoon onion powder

1 teaspoon garlic powder

¼ teaspoon ground black pepper

of the artichokes in the pot to keep them submerged. Simmer for 10 minutes. Remove from the heat and let the artichokes sit in the hot liquid for another 10 minutes. The artichokes are ready when a knife can be inserted with a little resistance. Remove the artichokes from the liquid and let sit at room temperature until they are cool enough to handle.

While the artichokes cool, in a small bowl, stir together the butter, Parmesan, remaining lemon zest, the onion powder, and the garlic powder to combine. Set aside.

Get the grill nice and hot.

Once the artichokes are cool, scrape away and discard the fuzz choke at the center of the artichoke heart with a spoon. Stuff the Parmesan butter in between the leaves, using all the butter (it may seem like a lot, but that's what you want). Season the stuffed artichokes with the remaining 1 teaspoon salt and the pepper. Grill them cut-side down until there are dark grill marks and the artichoke is slightly charred, 2 to 3 minutes. Turn them over and grill for another 2 minutes on the other side. Serve immediately or at room temp.

Note

⋆ These artichokes are great eaten as-is or served with a tangy lemon aioli for dipping the leaves. The Parmesan butter adds a lot of flavor and moisture, so dipping in aioli is a nice added touch, but these stand alone beautifully.

sweet potato jojos with buttermilk ranch dipping sauce

Prep Time: 10 minutes | Cook Time: 20 minutes

One day out of the blue, Olive decided that she hated Yukon gold potatoes, along with broccoli, egg yolks, and spinach! (This was also the day that she turned two, so I guess I shouldn't have been surprised. The mind of a toddler is a fickle thing.) With this new list of Olive's aversions in mind, I was trying to figure out alternative ways to make sure she was getting all the vitamins she needed. "JoJos" are pretty much just potato wedges coated in seasoned flour and then deep-fried, but there is not one ounce of frying in this recipe! There's a trick to getting the crispiest sweet potato oven fries: soaking the cut taters for at least 2 hours. So they require a bit of planning, but it's worth your time. It's *also* worth your time to make a homemade version of ranch dressing (it's so worthwhile, it appears twice in this book). Since my fickle two-year-old loved this recipe even in her most picky stages, it is officially "Olive approved."

Cut the sweet potatoes lengthwise into ½-inch-thick slices, then cut the slices into steak fries about 1 inch wide. Put the sweet potatoes in a large bowl or container and cover with cold water. Let sit at room temperature for at least 2 hours, or preferably overnight, to draw out the starch. Drain and rinse, then pat dry with paper towels.

In a small bowl, whisk ¼ cup of the milk and 2 teaspoons of the vinegar together. Let sit for 5 minutes. Add the mayo, sour cream, and ranch powder. Whisk thoroughly, then cover the dip and refrigerate until ready to serve (it will keep for up to 2 weeks).

Preheat the oven to 450°F. Line two baking sheets with parchment paper and spray with cooking spray.

MAKES 4 SERVINGS

2 large sweet potatoes, peeled (about 1½ pounds)

½ cup milk

1 tablespoon plus 2 teaspoons apple cider vinegar

¾ cup mayonnaise

½ cup sour cream

1½ tablespoons Ranch Powder (page 148)

Cooking spray

1 teaspoon olive oil

1 teaspoon garlic salt

½ teaspoon chili powder

½ teaspoon smoked paprika

½ cup all-purpose flour

Kosher salt, for serving

continued

sweet potato jojos with buttermilk ranch dipping sauce, continued

In a large bowl, whisk together the remaining ¼ cup milk and 1 tablespoon vinegar. Let sit for 5 minutes (use the time to gather the rest of your ingredients).

Add 2 tablespoons of water, the olive oil, garlic salt, chili powder, paprika, and flour to the milk and vinegar. Whisk to make a super-thick batter (it should be more of a paste than a batter). Add the sweet potato fries to the batter and toss with your hands, working the batter all over each fry to ensure even coating (gloves might be handy here).

Arrange the battered sweet potatoes on the prepared baking sheets in a single layer. Bake the fries for 15 minutes, then take them from the oven and carefully flip them over with a wide spatula. Return the pans to the oven and bake until the fries are deep brown, about 10 minutes more. Using a spatula, immediately transfer the fries to a wire rack to avoid them getting sweaty and soggy on the pan. Sprinkle with a little kosher salt and serve hot, with the ranch dip.

Notes

★ It seems like a fuss, but I always soak my sweet potatoes before making oven fries. Soaking draws out the extra starches that prevent the fries from getting super-crispy in the oven. If you can, soak them overnight, but soaking for at least 2 hours will do the trick. Be sure to drain and rinse them before proceeding with the recipe.

★ Use beer instead of water in the batter for beer-battered sweet potato fries. (The alcohol cooks off so it's fine for the kiddos).

★ Instead of going out and buying buttermilk, I like to make my own by mixing vinegar with regular milk and letting it sit for 5 minutes to thicken before combining with the other ingredients. If you happen to have buttermilk on hand, by all means use it in place of the milk and vinegar in both the ranch and the batter.

zucchini fritters with dilled cucumber salad

Prep Time: 10 minutes | Cook Time: 20 minutes

A (short-lived) low-carb kick that featured lots of zucchini led to the creation of these little fritters. Also, if you garden, you know that zucchini grow like they're on some sort of steroid, so you're always trying to figure out how to use them! Each Saturday and Sunday, I make brunch for whoever is home or visiting, and zucchini fritters are the perfect brunch food. They're great at room temperature, so you don't have to worry about rushing to serve everyone right away. I love to serve these as a crispy side dish or with some smoked salmon or poached eggs and hollandaise sauce (almost like a Benedict, but without the English muffin). The dilled cucumber salad is incredible on the fritters and the dish is a fabulous side with any protein you choose.

START THE SALAD: Cut the cucumber in half lengthwise and then cut it horizontally into thin half-moons. Put the cucumber slices in a medium bowl with the salt and massage them to release the water from the cucumber. Set aside.

MAKE THE FRITTERS: Combine the grated zucchini and potato in a strainer in the sink. Lay two or three paper towels on top and press the moisture out of the mixture, using your hands to squeeze the veggies from the top. They don't need to be squeezed completely dry, so don't go too crazy. Just squeeze until there is no longer a steady stream of liquid coming out of the bottom of the strainer. Put the squeezed veggies in a large bowl and add the dill, scallions, parsley, onion, garlic, salt, and pepper. Mix with your hands until well combined. Add the egg, baking powder, Tabasco, and flour. Mix with your hands until the batter is completely mixed and homogenous.

In a large skillet, heat the vegetable oil over medium-low heat. Scoop the fritter batter into the pan in small mounds, about 1½ tablespoons each, and use a spatula to flatten them into patties about 3 inches in diameter. Don't crowd the pan too

continued

MAKES 12 FRITTERS

For the salad

1 large English cucumber

½ teaspoon salt

¼ cup chopped fresh dill

¼ cup sour cream

1 teaspoon lemon zest

2 teaspoons fresh lemon juice

⅛ teaspoon ground black pepper

For the fritters

1 large zucchini, grated (about 1½ cups)

1 medium Yukon gold potato, rinsed and grated (about 1 packed cup)

½ cup fresh dill, coarsely chopped

3 scallions, chopped (about ½ cup)

½ cup coarsely chopped fresh parsley

½ medium red onion, grated (about ½ cup)

1 teaspoon minced garlic

1 teaspoon salt

1 teaspoon ground black pepper

1 egg, beaten

1 teaspoon baking powder

2 dashes of Tabasco sauce

¼ cup all-purpose flour

½ cup vegetable oil, plus more as needed

much; the fritters should have at least ½ inch between them. Fry until dark brown on the first side, 4 to 5 minutes, then gently flip them and cook until browned on the second side, 4 to 5 minutes more. Transfer the cooked fritters to a wire rack and repeat to cook the remaining batter. If the oil gets too low, top it off with another ¼ cup between batches and let it get hot before adding more batter.

MAKE THE SALAD: Pour the salted cucumbers into a strainer and lay two or three paper towels over the top. Press down with your hands, squeezing as much water as you can out of the cucumbers. Once the cucumbers are as dry as you can get them, transfer them to a medium bowl. Add the dill, sour cream, lemon zest, lemon juice, and pepper. Mix the salad until the cucumbers are well coated.

Top each fritter with a mound (about 1 tablespoon) of cucumber salad and serve.

Notes

- I'm not usually a big fried-food person, but it's pretty essential to use the generous amount of oil called for in this recipe. The crisp edges on these fritters are so amazing, and you can only get that by shallow-frying them.

- I use English cucumbers because they are crisp and sweet and I don't have to seed them.

- Try to get your potatoes squeezed and mixed as soon as you grate them. They will oxidize and turn brown really fast!

- Eat these as a side dish with chicken or fish or serve them with smoked salmon as fancy canapés.

dal-lish-ous lentils with ginger, garlic, and tomatoes

Prep Time: 30 minutes | Cook Time: 30 minutes

When our little Olive was on her way, my wife, Lesley, and I knew we wanted her to love *all* kinds of foods and flavors. We also didn't want to have to cook separate meals for her each time we ate. Family meals are important to us, and being a short-order cook for a picky child would take away from that. I made this Indian-inspired lentil dish for Olive and Lesley when I was (carefully) trying to see if Olive liked (or tolerated) strong flavors or hints of spice. Yep. I was *that* dad. My kitchen became a baby food testing lab! I was sure that introducing Olive to a wide variety of flavors early on would make for a much smoother family life—luckily, it worked for us, and so far she eats almost everything. Depending upon your mood, you may want to kick up the flavor of this dish with more garlic or more ginger. Others may want to dial back either (or both) ingredients.

Pour the boiling water over the lentils in a small bowl; set aside to soak for 30 minutes.

In a high-sided large sauté pan or casserole, heat the olive oil and coconut oil over medium-high heat. Add the onions, garlic, ginger, and jalapeño and sauté until the onions start to cook and become translucent, about 5 minutes.

Add the cherry tomatoes, cumin, garlic powder, bay leaves, cinnamon, turmeric, coriander, paprika, allspice, chili powder, and nutmeg and stir well with a wooden spoon. Cook over medium-high heat, stirring frequently and using the back of the spoon to smash the tomatoes into the spices and scrape the sides and bottom of the pot where the spices have started to stick and toast. Cook until the tomato juice has almost completely evaporated and the onions have completely cooked down, 11 to 12 minutes.

MAKES 4 TO 6 SERVINGS

2 cups boiling water

1 cup dried red lentils

2 tablespoons olive oil

2 tablespoons coconut oil

2 small to medium red onions, diced small (about 2 cups)

2 tablespoons minced garlic

2 tablespoons minced fresh ginger

1 large jalapeño, seeded and minced (about ¼ cup)

1 cup cherry tomatoes

1 teaspoon cumin seeds

1 teaspoon garlic powder

2 bay leaves

½ teaspoon ground cinnamon

½ teaspoon ground turmeric

½ teaspoon ground coriander

½ teaspoon paprika

½ teaspoon ground allspice

½ teaspoon chili powder

⅛ teaspoon ground nutmeg

1½ teaspoons kosher salt

2½ cups vegetable broth

½ bunch cilantro, coarsely chopped (about ½ cup)

1½ tablespoons lemon juice

continued

dal-lish-ous lentils with ginger, garlic, and tomatoes, continued

Pour the salt and broth into the pot and use the spoon to loosen any bits that have stuck to the bottom and sides of the pot. Drain the lentils and add them to the pot as well; give it a good stir. Reduce the heat to low and simmer, uncovered, stirring occasionally, until the lentils are cooked to al dente, about 20 minutes. Turn the heat off and remove the bay leaves. If you have an immersion blender, blend the mixture directly in the pot until about half the lentils are smooth. Otherwise, carefully scoop half the lentils into a blender or food processor and puree until smooth, then return the puree to the pot and stir to combine. Stir in the cilantro and lemon juice, and serve.

Notes

★ Instead of blending, you can mash half the lentils in the pot using a potato masher. It won't produce the same smooth result, but you will still have the half-mashed lentils to cream into the whole cooked lentils for a really delicious finished dish.

★ I like to eat this dish with a heaping scoop of plain yogurt mixed with a little sea salt and lemon juice to cut the spiciness.

olive oil yukon gold mashers

Prep Time: 5 minutes | Cook Time: 2 hours

MAKES 4 SERVINGS

4 pounds Yukon gold potatoes

1 tablespoon kosher salt

8 tablespoons (1 stick) unsalted butter, cubed

¼ cup plus 2 tablespoons olive oil

½ cup shredded Parmesan (2¾ ounces)

½ cup chopped fresh chives

½ teaspoon freshly cracked black pepper

In our house, we don't actually use a lot of butter, and living in California we are lucky to be surrounded by orchards of olive trees grown on big and small family farms. Olive oil is a great butter alternative, or it can be used in combination *with* butter as I do in this recipe. Olive oil also has amazing health benefits (and is good for your waistline). That said, if you end up wanting to add more butter, go for it. Oh, and don't skimp on the chives!

Cut the potatoes into approximately 2-inch chunks. Rinse in a colander and transfer to a large pot. Fill the pot with cold water to cover the potatoes by about 3 inches and bring to a boil over high heat. Add the salt and simmer over medium heat until the potatoes are just fork-tender, about 15 minutes. Drain the potatoes, reserving 1 cup of their cooking liquid.

Return the drained potatoes to the pot and add the butter and ¼ cup of the olive oil. Cover with a lid or kitchen towel and let sit for 3 to 5 minutes to melt the butter.

Add ¼ cup of the reserved cooking liquid and mash by hand with a potato masher or with a handheld mixer until smooth. (Save the remaining cooking liquid for any leftover potatoes; see Notes.) Transfer to a serving dish and sprinkle the Parmesan over the top. Drizzle with the remaining 2 tablespoons olive oil and top with the chives and cracked pepper just before serving.

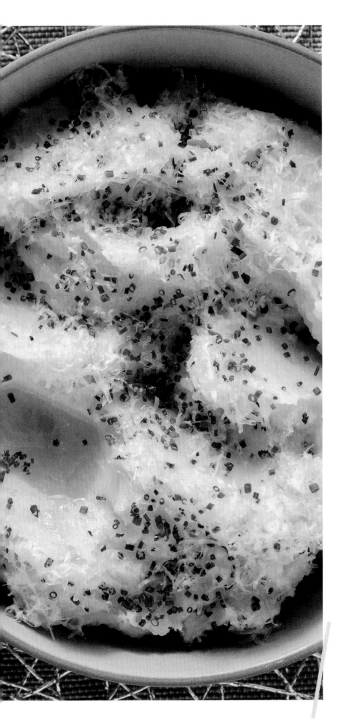

Notes

★ Don't worry about measuring your potatoes too precisely; just take 3 or 4 potatoes out of a 5-pound bag and you'll have close to 4 pounds.

★ Drain the boiled potatoes over a bowl, not in the sink! You'll need that cooking liquid to loosen up and store your mashers.

★ I like to make a huge batch of mashed potatoes and eat them all week (or more realistically, my wife and daughter eat them all week while I'm traveling for work) and have found the best way to store them is to pour a few tablespoons of the cooking liquid over the top of the potatoes in the container before refrigerating. That way, when we reheat them, they have that extra bit of liquid to help cream them out instead of being thick and gluey as leftover mashers can be sometimes.

★ If you're not afraid of the extra calories and you want to spoil yourself, use heavy cream or half-and-half instead of the cooking liquid when you mash.

★ The key to smooth mashers is making sure the potatoes are cut to the same size. They need to cook at the same rate—and don't overcook them, or you'll end up with potato soup.

year-round stuffing with shiitake mushrooms, leeks, and herbs

Prep Time: 15 minutes | Cook Time: 50 minutes

My young daughter is madly addicted to King's Hawaiian sweet rolls. Her excitement level over these is second only to the joy she shows when Mommy comes in the door after work. Food and pretty ladies . . . she really is a girl after my own heart! I feel the same way Olive does about those rolls *and* about stuffing. Luckily, King's Hawaiian bread has the perfect sweet and salty elements you want in a stuffing. It irritates me that we seem to think it is only acceptable to eat stuffing once a year! Here's one of my trade secrets when it comes to this recipe: I open a pack (of *rolls*, not of beer—the beer comes later, with the meal) and toast the whole thing. By using mushrooms and leeks, the dish becomes less holiday-ish and more of a year-round temptation. A fun tip: When the stuffing is leftover and cold, use an ice cream scoop to grab a ball of it, then place it on a hot griddle. You can sear it in the pan and serve it with poached or scrambled eggs. To make this the ultimate breakfast, ladle some sausage gravy over the top.

Preheat the oven to 400°F.

Separate the tops from the bottoms of the Hawaiian rolls, keeping the sheet intact. Put each half faceup on a baking sheet and drizzle 2 tablespoons of the olive oil on each half. Sprinkle ¼ teaspoon of the salt and ¼ teaspoon of the pepper over each half. Toast in the oven until deep dark brown (but not burnt), about 10 minutes. Tear the roll sheets into quarters and transfer to a large bowl, breaking them up just enough to fit into the bowl.

In a large sauté pan or casserole, heat ¼ cup of the olive oil over medium-high heat. Add the onion, celery, leek, and sage and sauté until the onion becomes translucent and the leek is fully cooked, about 10 minutes. Transfer the onion mixture to the bowl with the toasted bread.

MAKES 4 TO 6 SERVINGS

18 King's Hawaiian original sweet rolls

¾ cup olive oil

2½ teaspoons kosher salt

1½ teaspoons ground black pepper

1 large yellow onion, diced (about 2 cups)

2 cups diced celery (7 or 8 stalks)

3 leeks, white and very light green parts only, diced and rinsed well

1 bunch sage, finely chopped (scant ¼ cup)

4 cups sliced shiitake mushrooms (6 ounces)

1 tablespoon minced garlic

¾ cup chicken broth

4 tablespoons (½ stick) unsalted butter, plus more for greasing

1 bunch parsley, coarsely chopped (about 1 cup)

2 bunches scallions, sliced (about 1 cup)

continued

In the same pan, heat the remaining ¼ cup olive oil over medium heat. Add the mushrooms and garlic and sauté for 4 minutes, then add ¼ cup of water. Cook until the mushrooms are completely cooked, 2 to 3 minutes more. Transfer the mushroom mixture to the bowl with the toasted bread and onion mixture.

Reduce the oven temperature to 350°F. Butter a baking sheet.

In a small pot, bring the broth and butter to a boil. Add the remaining 2 teaspoons salt and 1 teaspoon pepper and stir to dissolve the salt. Pour the seasoned broth over the toasted bread and sautéed veggies in the bowl. Add the parsley and scallions. Using a wooden spoon, break the bread apart while mixing the stuffing together. I like big chunks of bread in my stuffing so I try not to break it up too much while I mix; when I'm done mixing there are still usually 2-inch chunks of bread.

Pour the stuffing into the prepared baking sheet, pressing down and evening it out to completely fill the sheet. Bake the stuffing on the top rack of the oven for 40 minutes, until nicely browned and crunchy on top. Serve it straight from the pan, or scoop it into a serving dish so that there are crunchy top bits mixed throughout.

Notes

- ⋆ If you prefer stuffing with a more traditional texture, chop up the rolls after toasting them.

- ⋆ Since this stuffing does not contain eggs, you could stuff the inside of a bird with it and not worry about it being undercooked.

- ⋆ If you don't have fresh sage, feel free to substitute 2 tablespoons dried sage and mix it with the broth instead of sautéing it with the veggies.

every-occasion potato salad with bacon-mustard vinaigrette

Prep Time: 15 minutes | Cook Time: 30 minutes

Looking through my list of recipes for this book, I wouldn't blame you if you worried that I might have a split personality! I jump around from vegan and salad recipes to full-fat recipes and red meats. But one thing I've learned in life is that there's a time to indulge and a time to have kale salads with dressings on the side. You have to have the yin with the yang. This is my non-mayo-based potato salad. I dress it with a tangy vinaigrette and with the bacon on top, and it is absolutely incredible. Like my mashed potatoes (see page 208) and a lot of my other veggie recipes, this recipe leans hard on good technique. Caramelizing the potatoes from top to bottom on a blistering-hot baking sheet is key. Adding the dressing while the potatoes are hot is the step that makes all the difference. It turns these spud sponges into a culinary flavor bomb.

Cut the bacon into ½-inch-wide pieces and cook in a large skillet over medium heat until evenly brown, crisp, and cooked. Drain the fat, reserving ¼ cup in the pan. Set the cooked bacon aside in a large bowl and leave the pan with the reserved fat on the stove with the heat turned off.

Rinse the potatoes and put them in a large pot with the salt. Add enough water to cover the potatoes by 2 inches, bring to a boil, and cook until fork-tender, 15 to 20 minutes. Drain the potatoes. If they are larger than bite-size, cut them in half or quarters.

Add the pepperoncini, mustards, vinegar, maple syrup, olive oil, and pepper to the bowl with the bacon and whisk until combined.

MAKES 4 SERVINGS

1 (12-ounce) package sliced bacon

2 pounds red, purple, and/or yellow creamer potatoes (the littlest ones you can find)

2 tablespoons salt

3 tablespoons chopped jarred pepperoncini

2 tablespoons whole-grain mustard

1 tablespoon Dijon mustard

2 tablespoons apple cider vinegar

1 tablespoon maple syrup

2 teaspoons olive oil

¼ teaspoon ground black pepper

½ cup chopped fresh chives

¼ cup chopped fresh parsley

continued

Heat the reserved bacon fat over high heat until melted and hot. Add the potatoes and, using a spatula, smash about one-third to half of them into the bacon fat. Reduce the heat to medium-high and cook the potatoes, undisturbed, until nicely browned, 3 to 4 minutes. Turn the heat off and pour the dressing over the potatoes in the pan. Add the bacon, chives, and parsley and gently toss to evenly coat the potatoes. Serve this potato salad warm or at room temp.

Note

If you store the potato salad in the fridge for later, try to bring it to room temp before serving; the flavors are more alive and vibrant at room temp than when cold.

coconut crispy rice

Prep Time: 2 minutes | Cook Time: 5 minutes

Happy accidents are some of the best things that can happen, and this is my accidental coconut rice. If you follow my grain grid on page 176, you'll likely end up with leftover grains. One night I was looking for a quick starch to make, and a jar of coconut oil was staring at me like the last bottle of red wine on a shelf at BevMo! So I heated a pan, got my oil smoking, then cooked rice until it was crunchy on one side (not both sides . . . this is not a stir-fry). Ever since then, it has been on our regular family menu. It's so simple to execute that I'm confident our dogs Pumpkin and Teddy could make this for us (although their lack of opposable thumbs might cause some issues)!

Heat a large nonstick skillet over medium-high heat. Pour in the coconut oil and heat until completely liquid and shimmering. Add the rice (straight from the fridge is fine, if you're using leftover rice—I usually do) and press it into the pan in a big even layer with a spatula. Cook, undisturbed, until nicely browned on the bottom, 3 to 5 minutes. Turn the heat off and give the rice a good stir, dispersing all the browned bits and the coconut oil throughout. Add the cilantro and lemon juice and gently fold until well mixed, being careful not to bruise the herbs. Serve immediately, with any protein or veg you like.

MAKES 4 SERVINGS

3 tablespoons coconut oil

2 cups cooked rice (preferably white; see grain grid, page 176)

½ bunch cilantro, coarsely chopped (about ½ cup loosely packed)

2 teaspoons lemon juice

Notes

* Different brands of coconut oil vary in intensity of coconut flavor. I think that it adds a great crispness to the rice, but I also love the subtle coconut flavor. Try a couple of brands and see what you prefer.

* I sometimes add chopped nuts, sliced scallions, toasted sesame seeds, toasted unsweetened coconut, or finely shredded kale or spinach.

* Try serving this rice with my 3/2/1 broiled chicken thighs (see page 117) and 3/2/1 broccoli (see page 191) for a quick weeknight dinner.

dessert

my almost-famous chocolate cream pie

Prep Time: 20 minutes | Cook Time: 45 minutes | Inactive Time: 2+ hours

**MAKES ONE 9-INCH
SINGLE-CRUST PIE**

Cooking spray, for greasing

1 disc On-the-Fly Pie Dough
(page 231)

All-purpose flour, for dusting

For the filling

5 large egg yolks, at room
temperature

3 tablespoons unsweetened
cocoa powder

¼ cup packed dark brown
sugar

1½ cups half-and-half

1½ teaspoons vanilla extract

½ teaspoon kosher salt

4 ounces milk chocolate,
coarsely chopped (⅔ cup)

4 ounces dark chocolate,
coarsely chopped (⅔ cup)

¼ cup light corn syrup

This chocolate pie has *no* clue how famous it *almost* was. Let me enlighten you: Once upon a time, I was cast on the hit Food Network show *Beat Bobby Flay,* where two chefs go head-to-head for the chance to (you guessed it) beat Bobby Flay! I went up against David Lebovitz, one of the best pastry chefs in the world. With all due respect to Mr. Lebovitz, I still think that *I* made the superior dish, but this recipe is called "*Almost* Famous" for a reason. I'm pretty sure you can guess the outcome. But luckily, this dessert is now famous in the *Scott* home. The On-the-Fly Pie Dough is the best pie crust recipe I've ever written, so if you just can't seem to make a decent pie crust, let mine boost your confidence. Fill it with chocolate, let it chill, and then fill your tummy one slice at a time.

PREPARE THE CRUST: Preheat the oven to 375°F. Spray a 9-inch pie dish with cooking spray.

Remove the disc of pie dough from the refrigerator and unwrap it. Roll out the dough on a well-floured surface into a 12-inch round. Carefully transfer the dough to the prepared pie dish. Using kitchen shears, trim the excess dough, leaving a ½-inch overhang around the edge. Tuck the overhanging dough under at the edge and gently press to seal the dough to the rim of the pie dish. Crimp the edge of the dough with your fingers or the tines of a large fork. Chill the pie shell in the freezer for 5 minutes.

Using a fork, prick the bottom of the dough all over. Line the dough with parchment or waxed paper and fill it with pie weights, dried beans, or uncooked rice. Bake until the crust is just shy of golden brown, 25 to 30 minutes. Carefully remove the parchment and weights and bake until the bottom of the crust is golden brown, about 5 minutes more. Let cool completely before filling.

continued

For the whipped cream

1¼ cups heavy cream

2 tablespoons packed brown sugar

1 tablespoon vanilla extract

1 dark chocolate bar, for garnish (and snacking)

MAKE THE FILLING: In a large bowl, whisk together the egg yolks, cocoa powder, and brown sugar until well combined.

In a medium saucepan, combine the half-and-half, vanilla, and salt and cook over medium-high until the mixture begins to simmer. While whisking continuously, slowly pour half the warm mixture into the egg mixture and whisk until combined, then scrape the warm egg mixture into the saucepan. Cook over medium heat, whisking continuously, until the custard has thickened, 2 to 3 minutes. Don't be worried if it looks slightly grainy or curdled.

Pour the hot custard into a food processor. Add the milk chocolate, dark chocolate, and corn syrup and process, stopping and scraping down the sides as necessary, until the chocolate has melted and the custard is smooth and velvety. Pour the custard into the pie crust and refrigerate for at least 2 hours or up to overnight. If leaving it overnight, cover the surface with plastic wrap to prevent a thick skin from forming. If you are trying to speed-chill it to eat that day, leave it uncovered to chill faster.

MAKE THE WHIPPED CREAM: In a large bowl, by hand or using an electric mixer, whisk together the cream, brown sugar, and vanilla until soft peaks form.

Dollop the whipped cream over the chocolate filling. Using a spoon or spatula, create decorative swirls, leaving a ½-inch border. Use a vegetable peeler on the dark chocolate bar or grate it on a microplane to create chocolate shavings directly over the top of the whipped cream for garnish.

Note

★ The longer the chocolate filling sets, the more firm it will be, but it will never get much firmer than a good thick chocolate pudding. Feel free to skip the crust and eat the filling (with whipped cream of course) straight out of a bowl!

brown butter butterscotch marshmallow square treats

Prep Time: 5 minutes | Cook Time: 10 minutes | Inactive Time: 1 hour 20 minutes

If I was on culinary "death row" and was allowed a last taste of my top three favorite ingredients, butterscotch would be one of them. Unlike much of the population, I don't go crazy for chocolate. But if a bowl of butterscotch chips were set in front of me, I'd look like Cookie Monster at a bakery's happy hour. This recipe—my stepped-up version of everyone's favorite childhood treat—is a nod to my mom, who taught me that simple can still be amazing. The ingredients list is short, and you may already have most of what you need sitting in your pantry. When friends drop by unexpectedly, open up a bottle of wine, pretend like this dessert took two hours to make, and tell everyone it's a secret recipe (and hope that they don't already own this book)!

Line the bottom and two sides of an 8-inch square cake pan with heavy-duty aluminum foil, leaving 2 inches of overhang on the two sides. Spray the foil and the exposed sides of the pan with cooking spray.

In a small saucepan, melt the butter over medium heat. Cook the butter, swirling the saucepan periodically to ensure the butter toasts evenly, until it turns a medium brown, 3 to 4 minutes. Immediately transfer the brown butter to a large glass bowl, along with any brown bits in the pan.

Add 3 cups of the marshmallows, the marshmallow crème, ½ cup of the butterscotch chips, and the salt to the bowl with the brown butter. Microwave in 30-second intervals, stirring after each, until the ingredients are melted and well combined, about 1½ minutes total.

Add the cereal and quickly stir to combine. Add the remaining marshmallows and remaining ½ cup butterscotch chips and quickly stir to combine. Be sure to work fast before the second addition of marshmallows and butterscotch melts and the mixture sets up.

continued

MAKES 9 GIANT BARS

Cooking spray, for greasing

4 tablespoons (½ stick) unsalted butter

1 (10-ounce) bag mini-marshmallows

1 (7-ounce) tub marshmallow crème (such as Fluff)

1 cup butterscotch chips

¼ teaspoon salt

6 cups crispy rice cereal

¼ cup dark chocolate chips

¼ teaspoon Maldon sea salt

Transfer the mixture to the prepared cake pan and use your hands to gently press it down, flattening the top. Let stand at room temperature for 1 hour, until cool and firm. Use the overhanging foil to lift the marshmallow treats out of the pan and set them on a cutting board; discard the foil.

Put the chocolate chips in a small glass bowl. Microwave the chocolate in 15-second intervals, stirring after each, until melted and smooth. Transfer the melted chocolate to a small zip-top bag. Cut a small hole in one corner of the bag and drizzle the chocolate over the top of the marshmallow treats in a grid pattern. Sprinkle the Maldon salt over the top and refrigerate until the chocolate has hardened, about 20 minutes. Cut the marshmallow treats into bars and serve.

Notes

- Keep an eye on that butter—it can go from brown to burnt in a flash!

- When combining the cereal, marshmallows, and butterscotch chips, be sure to work fast. As the marshmallow crème mixture cools, it will begin to thicken and be harder to work with.

- Spray your hands with some cooking spray when flattening the surface of the treats to keep the marshmallow crème from sticking to them.

lemon meringue pie with on-the-fly pie crust

Prep Time: 35 minutes | Cook Time: 1 hour | Inactive time: 3+ hours

**MAKES A 9-INCH
SINGLE-CRUST PIE**

For the pie crust

Cooking spray, for greasing

**1 disc On-the-Fly Pie Dough
(recipe follows), chilled**

All-purpose flour, for dusting

¼ cup white chocolate chips

1 tablespoon coconut oil

For the filling

¾ cup fresh lemon juice

1¼ cups sugar

**8 ounces (2 sticks) unsalted
butter, melted**

4 eggs

For the meringue

6 large egg whites

1½ cups sugar

¼ teaspoon cream of tartar

This pie crust is an adaptation and combination of my grandma's pie crust recipe and my friend Alan Carter's. Alan and I were classmates when I was earning my baking and pastry degree, and we bonded so well that we ended up working together at a restaurant later on in our careers. Alan was the person who taught me all about using vinegar in pie dough. That combo may sound super-strange, but you'll be amazed to see what a little bit of vinegar can do! It makes the dough tender by inhibiting gluten development and also makes it easier to work with, a well-kept secret (but maybe not anymore). Later, when I got a hold of Grandma's recipe, I learned that vinegar was her secret, too. This lemon meringue pie is something you'll want to make year-round. It is simple to create, and it will be a complete showstopper whenever (and wherever) it is served. Here's to you, Grandma Lena, and to my culinary brother, Alan! The cool (and interesting) trick that you both taught me over twenty years ago *finally* made it into one of my cookbooks!

PREPARE THE PIE CRUST: Spray a 9-inch pie dish with cooking spray.

Remove the disc of pie dough from the refrigerator and unwrap it. Roll out the dough on a well-floured surface into a 12-inch round. Carefully transfer the dough to the prepared pie dish. Using kitchen shears, trim the excess dough, leaving a ½-inch overhang around the edge. Tuck the overhanging dough under at the edge and gently press to seal the dough to the rim of the pie dish. Crimp the edge of the dough with your fingers or the tines of a large fork. Chill the pie shell in the freezer for 5 minutes.

Using a fork, prick the bottom of the dough all over. Line the dough with parchment or waxed paper and fill it with pie weights, dried beans, or uncooked

continued

rice. Bake until the crust is just shy of golden brown, 25 to 30 minutes. Carefully remove the parchment and weights and bake until the bottom of the crust is golden brown, about 5 minutes more. Let cool completely.

In a small bowl, combine the white chocolate and coconut oil and microwave in 15-second intervals, stirring after each, until the mixture is smooth, liquid, and well combined. Brush the cooled pie crust with the melted white chocolate mixture.

MAKE THE FILLING: Fill a medium pot halfway with water and bring the water to a boil.

In a medium heatproof bowl, whisk together the lemon juice, sugar, melted butter, and eggs. Set the bowl over the pot of boiling water (be sure the bottom of the bowl does not touch the water) and cook, whisking occasionally, until the lemon curd has thickened, 10 to 15 minutes. Remove the bowl from the pot but do not get rid of the boiling water—you'll need it for the meringue.

Pour the hot curd through a fine-mesh sieve into the prepared pie crust. Tap the pie on the counter gently to settle the curd and pop any air bubbles. Immediately put the pie in the fridge for 3 to 4 hours, until set (you can also put it in the freezer for 30 to 45 minutes to speed-chill it).

MAKE THE MERINGUE: In a clean metal bowl, whisk together the egg whites, sugar, and cream of tartar. Place the bowl over the pot of boiling water and leave it for 10 to 15 minutes, whisking occasionally. The egg white mixture should be hot to the touch and all the sugar should be dissolved. Pour the egg white mixture into the bowl of a stand mixer fitted with the whisk attachment and whip on high speed until it is cool and forms medium-stiff peaks (when you lift the whisk, the meringue should stand up in a peak, bend just at the tip). This should take about 20 minutes, so don't panic if it's not gaining volume right away.

Once the meringue is ready, pull the pie from the fridge or freezer. Turn the broiler on. You want the curd to be at least mostly set at this point so the meringue doesn't fall into the middle of the pie. Scoop the meringue into a gallon-size zip-top bag and cut off one corner so you have a large opening, about 1 inch. Starting at the edge of the curd filling and working your way in, pipe the meringue onto the pie. Once all the meringue is on the pie, use an offset spatula or the back of a spoon to create swirls and whorls in the meringue. Get creative and make it look as crazy (or perfect) as you like. The more spikes and swirls you have, the more interesting it will look once toasted.

Place the pie under the broiler, adjusting the rack as needed so the top of the meringue is a couple of inches from the heating element. Toast the meringue for 3 to 5 minutes, depending on the strength of your broiler. It will toast quickly, so keep an eye on it! You want it to be pretty golden brown everywhere, with the tips of the swirls a darker brown. Don't worry if it gets a little dark—it's just caramelized sugar, it will still taste just fine! Serve the pie right away or store it in the fridge and sneak pieces from it all week long.

Notes

- You can try substituting orange juice for the lemon juice in the filling for something different—just cut the sugar to ½ cup plus 2 tablespoons.

- Since this recipe is done in stages, you can prepare the individual components on different days to suit your schedule. Make the pie dough one day and the filling the next, then prepare the meringue and assemble the pie whenever you have the time.

- Just in case the curd is still a little jiggly in the middle and hasn't fully set up when you are topping it, piping the meringue from the edge working your way in will prevent the weight of the meringue from pushing the curd out of the pie from the center out.

- I paint the pie crust with melted white chocolate to seal it; the chocolate creates a barrier that prevents the curd from making it soggy. Cutting the white chocolate with coconut oil makes it more liquid and easier to brush.

- Since the meringue is cooked over boiling water before whipping, you don't need to worry about baking the meringue for very long. You just want to toast the top. Making the meringue this way results in more of a smooth marshmallow topping instead of a chunky, dry meringue.

continued

On-the-Fly Pie Dough

MAKES ENOUGH DOUGH FOR 2 SINGLE-CRUST PIES OR 1 DOUBLE-CRUST PIE

3 cups all-purpose flour

2 teaspoons kosher salt

2 teaspoons sugar

8 ounces (2 sticks) very cold unsalted butter, cubed

2 large egg yolks

1 tablespoon distilled white vinegar

½ cup ice water, plus more as needed

In a food processor, pulse the flour, salt, and sugar until combined. Add the butter and pulse until it is broken down into pea-size pieces, 5 to 8 pulses. Add the egg yolks and vinegar and pulse to combine, 3 or 4 pulses. Add the ice water ¼ cup at a time, pulsing 3 or 4 times after each addition, until the dough holds together. Test the dough by squeezing a small handful; if it does not easily hold together, add more ice water 1 tablespoon at a time, until it does.

Divide the dough in half (it will be crumbly) and place half on a sheet of plastic wrap. Pull the edges of the plastic wrap inward, pressing the dough onto itself to form a disc, then wrap the dough in the plastic wrap. Using a rolling pin, roll the dough to release any air pockets and to finish shaping it into a compact disc. Repeat with the remaining dough. Chill the disc(s) of dough in the refrigerator for at least 30 minutes before using. The dough can be stored in the fridge for up to 3 days or frozen for up to 1 month; thaw frozen dough in the fridge overnight before using.

foolproof gooey brownies

Prep Time: 5 minutes | Cook Time: 30 minutes

MAKES ONE 8-INCH SQUARE PAN

Cooking spray, for greasing

1¼ cups semisweet chocolate chips

8 tablespoons (1 stick) unsalted butter

¼ cup light corn syrup

1 cup sugar

¾ cup all-purpose flour

⅓ cup unsweetened cocoa powder (see Note)

¾ teaspoon baking soda

½ teaspoon salt

2 eggs

Note

★ Make sure you use natural cocoa powder, not Dutch-process cocoa. Dutch-process cocoa has been alkalized and won't react with the baking soda.

It was not until fifteen years after culinary school that I learned the best (and easiest) trick to making gooey brownies. Bringing the butter and sugar to a boil and using it to melt the chocolate is the game-changing step! If you don't believe me (and you skip that part), please don't tell anybody that this was *my* gooey brownie recipe. It will undoubtedly fall short of the name's expectations. I'd be naive to think that you won't tell people it's *your* recipe, so go ahead and claim it. This is truly a simple, no-fuss, straight-up gooey brownie that you can be proud of making from scratch. Feel free to add walnuts, pecans, or macadamia nuts if you like. Making a double batch of brownies is always a good idea, too—just be sure to use two separate pans (unless you like a giant lump of overcooked-on-the-outside-but-raw-on-the-inside chocolate). Bake these ahead and freeze them so you have them on hand for company . . . or for those late-night chocolate cravings.

Preheat the oven to 325°F. Grease an 8-inch square baking dish with cooking spray.

Put the chocolate chips in a large bowl.

In a small saucepan, melt the butter over medium-low heat. Add ¼ cup of water, corn syrup, and sugar and stir to combine. Bring the mixture to a boil, then immediately pour it over the chocolate. Whisk until the chocolate has completely melted. Add the flour, cocoa powder, baking soda, and salt and whisk to combine. Add the eggs and whisk until the batter is thoroughly mixed.

Pour the batter into the prepared pan and even it out with a spatula. Bake for about 40 minutes, until a toothpick inserted into the center comes out a little gooey but the edges are firm. The brownies will have puffed up considerably, then fallen back down, creating a high crust and a well in the middle. By the time it cools down, the carryover heat will have cooked the center to exactly the right gooey (yet cooked) consistency, with perfectly chewy edges.

everything-but-the-kitchen-sink cookies

Prep Time: 10 minutes | Cook Time: 7 minutes

This is one cookie that Lesley's girlfriends always ask for when they come over. I never mind giving out my recipes to friends, but what cracks me up is that they never want the *recipe*—they just want me to make the cookies *for* them! The cereal and salty snacks I've called for can be swapped out for similar kinds, but other than that, you'll have to trust me and follow my lead. Coffee, coconut, and cornflakes really *do* go together! I know, #DoubtersGonnaDoubt. Bake a batch of these cookies on a Sunday when you're already planning to go to the gym the next morning, because you will undoubtedly eat all of them. You can also toss some in the freezer for a go-to anytime dessert for your family (or company). Just know that if your patience is anything like mine, you may settle for just eating them straight out of the freezer!

Preheat the oven to 375°F. Line two baking sheets with parchment paper.

In the bowl of a stand mixer fitted with the paddle attachment or in a large bowl using a handheld mixer, cream the butter, brown sugar, and granulated sugar on low speed until smooth. Add the eggs and vanilla and mix on low speed until smooth and homogenous. Stop and scrape down the sides of the bowl. Add the flour, salt, and baking soda and mix on low speed until smooth and completely combined. Add the peanut butter chips, pretzels, potato chips, rice cereal, cornflakes, coconut, and coffee. Mix on low speed until just combined. If you overmix the dough, the chips and pretzels will get too crushed to be recognizable in the cookies.

MAKES 48 COOKIES

1 cup (2 sticks) unsalted butter, at room temperature

1¾ cups lightly packed light brown sugar

½ cup granulated sugar

2 eggs

2 teaspoons vanilla extract

1½ cups all-purpose flour

1 teaspoon salt

1 teaspoon baking soda

1 cup peanut butter chips

1 cup pretzel sticks, crushed a little by hand to fit into the measuring cup

1 cup potato chips, crushed enough to measure into a cup

1 cup crispy rice cereal

1 cup cornflakes

¾ cup unsweetened shredded coconut

3 tablespoons ground coffee

continued

Using a mounded tablespoon or 1-ounce ice cream, scoop the dough onto the prepared baking sheets, spacing the cookies 2 inches apart. Bake until the edges are brown and the centers are still a little pale, 6 to 7 minutes. Repeat to bake the remaining cookie dough.

Let cool completely, then store in an airtight container or zip-top bag at room temperature for up to 5 days.

Notes

⭐ This is really a "clean out your cupboards" cookie recipe, so feel free to substitute any leftover sweet or salty snacks you have laying around that might go well in a cookie: candied nuts, salted nuts, chopped candy bars, popcorn, etc.

⭐ The high ratio of brown sugar in this dough makes it super-chewy and almost caramelly. It's the best base for almost any drop cookie, from chocolate chip to blueberry-coconut.

⭐ To up the savory-sweet ante, press a hearty pinch of crushed potato chips and pretzels into the top of each cookie before baking.

⭐ Bake this dough the day you make it; refrigerating it to bake later gives the pretzels time to absorb moisture and get soggy.

super-soft frosted birthday cake cookies

Prep Time: 10 minutes | Cook Time: 15 minutes

This is the cookie for adults who find themselves getting jealous watching a one-year-old devour their own personal-size smash cake. It's also the perfect recipe for the adult who wants their birthday to last as *long* as possible. For example, my mom believes in a birthday *month* instead of a birthday *day*. And if you're like me, you want to eat birthday cake more than once a year (not that I want to get *older* twice a year). Maybe I should have called these "Honey I Shrunk the Cake" cookies. All the birthday cake flavor is there! I made these for Olive's first and second birthdays (and for her un-birthdays as well). They're my favorite kind of cookie. So, whip up a batch and celebrate any random Monday (or silly made-up holiday). You should never need a reason to want to celebrate *something*.

MAKE THE COOKIES: Preheat the oven to 350°F. Line two baking sheets with parchment paper.

In a large bowl using a handheld mixer or in the bowl of a stand mixer fitted with the paddle attachment, cream the butter, granulated sugar, baking powder, and salt until fluffy, 3 to 4 minutes.

In a small bowl, whisk together the egg whites, cream, and vanilla until well combined.

With the mixer running on low speed, add the liquid mixture in three stages, stopping to scrape the bowl down after each addition. Beat the mixture for 2 minutes, until fluffy.

Add the flour and mix on low speed just until combined. Scrape down the sides of the bowl and mix on low speed for 1 minute more.

MAKES 48 COOKIES

For the cookies

8 ounces (2 sticks) unsalted butter, at room temperature

1 cup granulated sugar

2 teaspoons baking powder

1¼ teaspoon salt

2 large egg whites

2 tablespoons heavy cream

2 teaspoons vanilla extract

2¼ cups bleached cake flour, sifted (see Note)

For the frosting

2 cups confectioners' sugar

¼ cup heavy cream

1 teaspoon vanilla extract

¼ teaspoon salt

3 or 4 drops food coloring (Olive likes pink)

2 to 3 tablespoons fun colorful sprinkles

continued

Scoop the cookie dough by rounded tablespoons onto the prepared baking sheets, keeping 3 inches between each cookie. Make sure the scoops are very round; a small ice cream scoop works well for this. Bake the cookies for 12 to 15 minutes. They should have almost no color on top, and just the lightest bare amount of light browning at the edges. Let the cookies cool completely on the baking sheets; do not move them to a wire rack for cooling. Repeat with the remaining cookie dough.

MAKE THE FROSTING: In a medium bowl using an electric hand mixer, beat the confectioners' sugar, cream, vanilla, salt, and food coloring on low speed until the sugar has been fully dissolved by the liquid. Scrape down the bowl and beat the frosting on high speed until light and fluffy.

When the cookies are cool, frost each one with a tablespoon (or more!) of the fluffy vanilla frosting. Use a butter knife or small offset spatula to create a swirl in the frosting on top of each cookie. Sprinkle the frosted cookies with colorful sprinkles. The frosting will form a little bit of a skin as it sits, so be sure to add the sprinkles right away so they stick. Store these cookies in an airtight container at room temperature for 3 to 4 days. Be sure not to stack them directly on top of each other so that the icing stays pretty.

Notes

* Sift the cake flour after measuring for a more accurate measurement.

* These cookies are almost more cake than cookie, kind of like handheld mini-birthday cakes.

* It may seem like you're using a *lot* of vanilla and salt, but trust me, these two ingredients are what make this cookie stand out and give them a flavor so reminiscent of the grocery-counter favorite we all grew up loving.

insanely delicious vegan and gluten-free double chocolate cookies

Prep Time: 5 minutes | Cook Time: 9 minutes

MAKES 24 COOKIES

⅔ cup coconut oil, at room temperature but solid, not liquid (see Notes)

⅔ cup lightly packed light brown sugar

½ cup granulated sugar

½ cup unsweetened almond milk

2½ cups gluten-free all-purpose flour, such as Cup4Cup

½ cup unsweetened Dutch-processed or extra-dark cocoa powder

1 teaspoon salt

1 teaspoon baking soda

½ teaspoon baking powder

2 cups vegan dark chocolate chunks

2 tablespoons Maldon sea salt

If you don't tell people these cookies are gluten-free and vegan, they'll *never* know. Coconut oil replaces butter or shortening, with amazing results. Since the dough is brown from the cocoa powder, it will be difficult to tell if they are sufficiently browned just by looking, so keep an eye on that timer, and please, bake them for nine minutes and nine minutes *only*. The exact baking time is key in avoiding hard, dry cookies. I love leaving a bunch of these on the counter for the girls to enjoy when I have to leave for a work trip. It's my "so sorry I'm gone but scarf on these and you'll forgive me" plan, and it has yet to fail me!

Preheat the oven to 350°F. Line two baking sheets with parchment paper.

In a medium bowl using an electric mixer, cream the coconut oil, brown sugar, and granulated sugar until fluffy, 3 to 4 minutes. Add the almond milk and mix on medium speed until fully incorporated. Scrape down the sides of the bowl and mix for 1 minute more. Add the flour, cocoa powder, salt, baking soda, and baking powder. Mix on low speed until all the ingredients are incorporated and well mixed. Add 1½ cups of the chocolate chunks and mix by hand until they are evenly distributed. Scoop 2-tablespoon mounds of the dough onto the prepared baking sheets, spacing the cookies at least 2 inches apart. Press the remaining chocolate chunks onto the tops of the cookie dough balls and sprinkle a small pinch of Maldon salt onto each one. Bake for 9 minutes. When you gently touch the center of a cookie, it should be soft and won't spring back, but it won't be liquid or jiggly.

Let cool completely on the pans. Store in an airtight container or zip-top bag at room temperature for up to 5 days.

Notes

★ It's important that the coconut oil is solid, but at room temperature. Coconut oil liquefies at warm room temp, so if it's liquid in your cupboard, pop it in the fridge for a minute to firm it up. (Conversely, you don't want it rock hard from the fridge, because it will be difficult to cream with the sugars.)

★ If you don't need these to be gluten-free, go ahead and use regular all-purpose flour.

★ When measuring the cocoa powder, be sure to scoop the cocoa into the measuring cup before leveling it off with a spatula. Scooping the cocoa with the measuring cup will result in too much cocoa for this recipe.

follow-me-everywhere butterscotch pudding

Prep Time: 5 minutes, plus 4 hours cooling | Cook Time: 15 minutes

Other than Olive, this recipe is my *baby!* I learned a surprising fact about myself while I was in culinary school: I'm not a chocolate lover. I thought that someday I *would* be, but nope. In 2001, while working toward my pastry chef degree, I learned about all the differences between bittersweet, milk, and dark chocolates, and the differences between various *kinds* of dark chocolate (60% cacao versus 40%, etc.). Even after trying every kind of chocolate you could imagine, I never felt those sparks. Butterscotch, on the other hand, will always have my heart. This pudding was a best seller in all four of my restaurants over the years and has been on every menu. You can serve this no matter the season, and at any holiday or gathering—it will blow people's socks off! I top it with whipped cream and chocolate shavings for some extra pizzazz.

PS: To "adult-ify" it, add a touch of bourbon for a next-level experience.

PPS: Pour this pudding into ice pop molds, stick them in the freezer, and you'll have pudding pops for the kiddos in no time!

In a small bowl, whisk together the gelatin and milk; set aside to bloom while you make the butterscotch mixture.

In a large pot, melt the butter over low heat. Add the brown sugar and salt. Increase the heat to medium-high and cook, stirring continuously, until the mixture is smooth and the color turns from gold to brown, 5 to 7 minutes. Turn the heat off and, while whisking continuously, very slowly and carefully pour in the half-and-half. (Be careful of the steam that comes up when you pour the half-and-half; pour a little at a time.) Return the pot to high heat and whisk until there are no sugar solids left and the mixture is almost at a boil.

continued

MAKES 8 SERVINGS

2 (¼-ounce) packets unflavored powdered gelatin

½ cup cold milk

8 tablespoons (1 stick) unsalted butter

1¾ cups lightly packed light brown sugar

1 teaspoon salt

4¾ cups half-and-half

5 egg yolks

1 cup butterscotch chips

Whipped cream, for serving

Chocolate shavings, for serving (see Note)

In a medium bowl, whisk the egg yolks to break them up. While whisking continuously, slowly pour 1 cup of the hot caramel mixture into the yolks, then whisk to combine. Pour the yolk mixture into the pot and whisk to combine. Cook over medium heat until the mixture comes to a simmer. Turn the heat off, add the butterscotch chips, and whisk until they have melted completely. Add the bloomed gelatin-milk mixture and whisk to combine. Strain the hot pudding through a fine mesh strainer into a glass baking dish or heatproof bowl. Press a sheet of plastic wrap directly against the surface of the pudding to prevent a skin from forming and refrigerate until cool and firm, at least 4 hours and up to 4 days.

Before serving, beat the pudding with a rubber spatula or wooden spoon. The gelatin will have firmed it up quite a bit, but with a little muscle, it will smooth right out. You can also put it in your food processor or stand mixer. If you do, it will seem a little too runny at first, but it will firm right back up as it sits, so don't worry. Scoop the pudding into serving cups, top with whipped cream and chocolate shavings, and serve.

Notes

- Try this as a pie! Slice a couple of bananas and line the bottom of a graham cracker crust with them. Pour the pudding into the crust and top the pie with whipped cream and chocolate shavings.

- To make your own chocolate shavings, use a vegetable peeler to shave off delicate curls from a large bar of dark chocolate.

throwback pink snowballs

Prep Time: 30 minutes, plus 1+ hour chilling | Cook Time: 6 minutes

Pink snowball cakes are so nostalgic! The originals, along with Little Debbie snack cakes, whoopie pies, and Hostess Zingers, were staples in every 1970s or '80s convenience store. Ever since graduating pastry school in 2000, one of my goals has been to re-create foods and sweet treats from my childhood, which is why I've included my butterscotch pudding (see page 245), gooey brownies (see page 232), these pink snowballs, and other memory-rich recipes in this book. When I serve these, I like to play a fun little game with my guests, one you may want to give a try, too: I put these pink cakes on a platter and set them out without any explanation. Then I wait in anticipation for my guests' reactions! I am never disappointed. They either have *no* idea what they're looking at, or they recognize them right away and are absolutely *tickled* by seeing a homemade version of this classic treat. I'm now having to teach my daughter (and my Gen Z staff) what a "pink snowball" is, but I'll gladly eat twelve just to show them.

MAKE THE CAKE: Preheat the oven to 350°F. Spray two or three nonstick mini-muffin tins (for 36 mini-muffins total) with cooking spray.

In a large bowl, whisk together the granulated sugar, flour, cocoa powder, baking powder, baking soda, and salt until well mixed.

Add the eggs, buttermilk, and coffee and mix until smooth. Scrape down the sides of the bowl, then add the melted butter and whisk until smooth and well combined.

Scoop the batter into the prepared mini-muffin tins, filling each cup three-quarters full. Bake until the tops bounce back when pressed lightly, 5 to 6 minutes. Let cool in the tins for 10 minutes, then turn the cupcakes out onto a plate and refrigerate until they firm up.

continued

MAKES 36 MINI-SNOWBALL CAKES

For the cupcakes

Cooking spray, for greasing

1 cup plus 2 tablespoons granulated sugar

¾ cup plus 2 tablespoons all-purpose flour

½ cup unsweetened Dutch-process cocoa powder

1¼ teaspoons baking powder

½ teaspoon baking soda

¼ teaspoon salt

2 eggs

⅓ cup buttermilk

¼ cup brewed coffee

5 tablespoons unsalted butter, melted

throwback pink snowballs, continued

MAKE THE FILLING AND FROSTING: In the bowl of a stand mixer fitted with the paddle attachment or in a medium bowl using an electric hand mixer, beat the butter until smooth. Add the marshmallow crème and beat until smooth.

Add the salt, then add the confectioners' sugar in two stages (to prevent it from flying everywhere as you mix) and mix on low speed until all the sugar is moistened. Increase the speed to high and beat until fluffy. Add the vanilla and beat until fully incorporated.

Line a baking sheet with parchment paper. Pour the coconut onto the baking sheet. Wearing gloves, apply a couple of drops of food coloring to one palm. Rub your palms together to cover them with food coloring, then scoop up the coconut and rub it between your hands to tint the coconut pink. Continue scooping and rubbing the coconut until you've colored all the coconut completely. Set aside.

ASSEMBLE THE SNOWBALLS: Take the cupcakes out of the fridge and turn them upside-down. Trim any overhang from the rims of the cupcakes so they are clean and even.

Poke a hole in the flat bottom of each cupcake (which will be facing up since they are upside-down) with a paring knife and wiggle the knife around a little to make room for the filling.

Scoop the frosting into a plastic piping bag (or use a small zip-top bag and cut off about ¼ inch from one corner). Pipe the frosting into the hole in each cupcake, filling them as much as you can without splitting them.

Pipe the frosting all over the outside of each filled cupcake, creating a domed shape. Don't worry if it's not perfect—you'll be able to fix the shape once the coconut is on. Just make sure each cupcake is mostly covered with frosting.

For the filling and frosting

8 tablespoons (1 stick) unsalted butter, at room temperature

1 (7-ounce) tub marshmallow crème (such as Fluff)

¼ teaspoon salt

2 cups confectioners' sugar

1½ teaspoons vanilla extract

1 (12-ounce) bag sweetened shredded coconut

3 or 4 drops red or pink food coloring

continued

throwback pink snowballs, continued

Using a cake spatula or butter knife, place a frosted cupcake onto the baking sheet with the coconut. Cover the cupcake with coconut, using your hands to press it against the frosting to adhere. Once the cupcake is covered with coconut, gently pick it up and use your hand to form it back into a dome shape. Place it gently on a serving platter or a clean baking sheet lined with parchment paper. Repeat to coat the rest of the cupcakes.

Serve the snowballs right away, or store them in an airtight container at room temperature for up to 4 days.

Notes

* You can fill and frost the cupcakes at room temp, but it is much easier and cleaner to do it when they are firm from the fridge.

* Don't worry about shaping these into perfect little domes or if the frosting spills out when you fill them. Once they are covered with the frosting and shredded coconut, you can easily shape them into cute little dome shapes.

* Feel free to skip the dome shapes altogether and just fill and frost these as regular mini-cupcakes with coconut on top! The key is getting the kids in on it and having a good time (and eating delicious treats while doing it, of course).

hummingbird bundt cake with cream cheese glaze

Prep Time: 15 minutes, plus 1 hour cooling | Cook Time: 45 minutes

MAKES ONE 10-INCH BUNDT CAKE OR 12 MINI (3-INCH) BUNDT CAKES

For the cake

Cooking spray or vegetable oil, for greasing

1 cup unsweetened shredded coconut

¼ cup dark rum

2 cups all-purpose flour

1 cup granulated sugar

1 cup lightly packed light brown sugar

2 teaspoons ground cinnamon

1 teaspoon ground ginger

1 teaspoon baking soda

1 teaspoon salt

1½ cups vegetable oil

¼ cup molasses

4 eggs

1 cup drained canned diced pineapple

1 cup small-diced bananas (2 to 3 bananas)

1 cup pecan pieces

This cake recipe is another nod to my southern grandma, Lena. She may have passed, but her influences live on in my recipes. Maybe it's just me, or maybe because of where I grew up, but I seriously thought pineapples grew in a can and came chunked or spiraled straight from nature. Today I like to say that canned foods have a place in our life (mostly when we're camping or in quarantine)—and without canned pineapple, this cake would suffer a major identity crisis. Even though this cake is packed with fruit and nuts, I promise you, it is light, fluffy, and downright heavenly! I serve this southern-inspired treat at Thanksgiving, Christmas, or Easter as an alternative dessert to the standard pie. Just make sure you have copies of the recipe printed out for the impending requests. Your hand will get tired of writing it out on party napkins and paper plates.

MAKE THE CAKE: Preheat the oven to 325°F. Grease a 10-inch Bundt pan or 8 mini (4-inch) Bundt pans with cooking spray, or brush with vegetable oil. Make sure to grease the center tube all the way up to the top—this is the part that sticks the most.

In a small microwaveable dish, combine the coconut, ¼ cup of water, and rum. Microwave on high for 30 seconds, then set aside while you make the cake batter.

In a large bowl, combine the flour, granulated sugar, brown sugar, cinnamon, ginger, baking soda, and salt. Add the oil, molasses, and eggs and stir until well combined, making sure there are no clumps of flour. Add the pineapple, bananas, rum-soaked coconut, and pecan pieces and fold the batter until the ingredients are mixed evenly. Pour the batter into the prepared pan, making sure to leave at least 2 inches at the top of the pan for rising (see Note). Bake until the cake is fragrant and deep brown and springs back when you gently touch the top, 45 to 50 minutes (for mini-cakes, reduce the baking time to 20 minutes). A skewer inserted into the center of the cake should come out mostly clean, with

continued

hummingbird bundt cake with cream cheese glaze, continued

For the glaze

½ (8-ounce) package full-fat cream cheese, at room temperature

4 tablespoons (½ stick) unsalted butter, at room temperature

½ teaspoon vanilla extract

1 cup confectioners' sugar

just a few moist crumbs clinging to it. Let the cake cool in the pan for 20 to 30 minutes before unmolding.

To unmold the cake, run a paring knife around just the top edge of the cake and around the center tube. Place a plate on top of the pan and invert the plate and pan together. Give the cake a firm knock on the counter to loosen it, then gently remove the pan. Let the cake cool completely, at least 1 hour, before glazing.

MAKE THE GLAZE: In a large bowl using a handheld mixer or whisk, beat the cream cheese and butter until creamy. (You can do this by hand, but it's much easier with an electric mixer.) Add the vanilla and confectioners' sugar and mix slowly so the sugar is absorbed without flying everywhere. Once the sugar has been absorbed, beat the glaze until smooth, 2 to 3 minutes more.

Gently heat the glaze until it is liquid and pourable but still thick, either microwaving it in 10-second increments or setting the bowl over a saucepan of simmering water. Pour the liquid glaze over the top of the cooled cake, letting it drip down the sides. Serve immediately, or let the glaze firm up. This cake will last, covered and stored at room temperature, for 3 to 4 days.

Notes

★ When filling a large Bundt pan, leave 2 inches at the top. If you are using minis, fill them slightly more than three-quarters full.

★ Instead of microwaving the coconut to speed-soak it, you can bring the rum and water to a boil and then immediately pour it over the coconut. You'll still need to let it sit for at least 20 minutes while you get the batter together.

★ If you're using a Bundt pan that has a very intricate design, you may have some leftover batter (sometimes the more heavily designed pans have less capacity). If so, just bake the rest of the batter in muffin tins or a small loaf pan. Don't fill your Bundt pan more than three-quarters full, or you may end up with a big mess in your oven.

★ You can garnish the glazed cake with chopped pecans, chopped dried pineapple, or toasted coconut, if you like.

acknowledgments

I would like to congratulate my team and award them an honorary, gilded bottle of Tito's vodka for accomplishing the unimaginable: writing and publishing a book during a global pandemic! We delivered ahead of schedule even with children hanging on our legs and popping into our Zoom conference calls! We juggled managing our personal lives, maintaining social distancing, home-schooling kids, cancelling in-person work sessions, and moving all meetings to electronic ones—all while dealing with our own stresses during this trying time. My incredible team took a deep breath, re-evaluated, made adjustments, and just GOT IT DONE. Between Dana's drive for perfection, Cheryl's OCD-ness, and Chris Andre's commitment to not let six feet of distance keep us from getting the most clutch, close-up photos for this book, the result is a project that I am so proud to see come to fruition . . . despite the insane challenges!

My "baby burrito," Olive: This should be easy, but how do I give enough credit to the little person who absolutely changed our lives and made all of our dreams come true? Your smiles, joy, zest for life, and endless love for everyone around you has a magic way of making me hit the "reset button," bringing me back to what really matters. This book is for you and for Mommy. Daddy loves you, always and forever.

Lesley: It did not take a pandemic to make me understand how important you are, and always have been to me. I have known it since the first day that I met you. When it came to meeting the love of my life, my mother always told me "you'll know." If the fact that we moved in together after just three months of dating does not prove those words to be true, I don't know what would! You are the glue that keeps our lives together. My life didn't truly start until nine years ago when we met. Thank you for being the most incredible mom to Olive and for being my love, and my best friend.

My mother, Pat, aka "Mama Pat:" You are the person who keeps our family at-large ticking and sane through your love and support. You taught me that with an open heart (and a big plate of cookies), you can fix anything. I am forever grateful for you and your endless love as a mom and grandma, and for your encouragement in all of my endeavors. Danny: A lot of stepfathers enter into that role with reservation, but you jumped in with both feet and a big smile on your face. As a father, grandfather, great friend, and confidant, you are second-to-none. I love you and the way you love our family. Thank you for always being there for us. Michael Eldridge: You are my father-in-law, but also one of my best friends (and a great drinking buddy too). Thanks for your friendship, support, and constant reminder to live for today. Here's to many more drinks and road trips. I love you, buddy. Bonnie Eldridge: My mother-in-law with a heart of gold. You endearingly say that recipes are made of a "little bit of this and a little bit of that" and this book echoes your words throughout. You are an amazing mom, grandma, and friend. This time I hope that you realize that I mentioned you in the acknowledgments before multiple years have passed!

Sheri: This book would not have happened without you. Your constant and selfless love and support (as well as being an amazing auntie and my wife's best friend) have kept our family running smoothly.

Dana Baker: Not only are you a dear friend, but you are a creative force to be reckoned with! You single-handedly carried this book from the beginning to end. You spoiled me with your attention to details throughout the creative process. You executed your work at the highest level. Thanks again, buddy. You did it!

Cheryl Storms: There is not a better person than you in the culinary world. You signify and stand up for what the culinary arts field should be. Your sass has kept me on my toes for almost a decade and I am honored to call you one of my closest friends and right-hand-woman. I love you, "fancy pants" aka "heavy cream."

Kirsten Neuhaus and Foundry Literary+ Media: You championed this book from its conception and gave this project its legs. You steamrolled it through all of the hurdles that stood in our way. Your foresight and optimism will have us publishing books together for years to come. Thank you from the bottom of my heart.

Justin and Stephanie and the whole team at Houghton Mifflin Harcourt: I feel incredibly spoiled to have worked with both of you. You have believed in me and this book since day one. To work with publishers such as yourselves has allowed our creativity to flow without restraint. Stephanie, you are amazing, and this book truly came to life through your encouragement and careful direction. Thank you so much.

Chris Andre: You are hands-down one of the most crazy-talented people I have ever had the privilege to work with. You tolerated my 6'3" frame looming over your shoulder and my constant changing of sets while I kept whispering "what do you think?" in your ear. Four hundred frames later, we have arrived at this place and I could not be any prouder. I can't thank you enough.

Esteban Baes: My amazingly talented chef and good friend. You can now add "food stylist" to your resume! You jumped in with an open heart (and face-mask-ready), eager to share your talents while doing things that you had never tried before (and in a completely new way)! Thanks for lending your amazing talent to this cookbook. I love you, buddy.

Steve Hernandez: My "therapist" and best friend. You are my mentor and first chef. I am beyond honored to call you my best friend, drinking buddy, and one of the only people who can listen to Dwight Yoakam with me for twenty-four hours straight and not get annoyed!

Zach Schiffman: I wish I had met you twenty years ago because your friendship is so incredible! When my phone goes off at 6am I always know that it is you with some goofy GIF to brighten my morning. Thanks for bringing me laughs, smiles, and love . . . and for bringing joy to my family (and now to your family) as well.

Rachael Ray: I have looked up to you for years and now you are a dear friend, confidant, mentor, and so much more. Thanks for your continued support and for being a big fan of mine. You know I am your biggest fan. I love you, Rach.

Carla Hall: You are a dear friend and have been an important part of my culinary (and life's) journey! I am so thankful that Top Chef brought us together and I continue to be inspired by your incredible spirit and your culinary expertise. You are magical. Thank you for sharing your friendship with me and for graciously (and expertly) writing the foreword. Your keen perspective and infectious joy were just what this book needed as its introduction! Big hugs, my dear.

Hoda Kotb: We go way back! Through almost a decade and a half of TV I feel honored to have even been a small part of your television journey as I have cooked beside you. We have evolved together from living lives as single people, to becoming parents and living our best lives. I want to take this opportunity to say thank you for your endless support, true friendship, and for your bright smile that has always encouraged me and everyone you connect with each day. Thanks for being you.

Wes: Two years ago we lost you, my best friend and brother. Olive was just six months old, but your presence still resonates, illuminating and guiding us in the Scott home. When you passed, Les and I brought your last houseplant home with us. Ever since, Olive and I have watered it together every morning. Soon she'll understand that it is our own special piece of "Uncle Wes." It stands strong, reaching for the sun, reminding us that we all have something to live for when we are always looking for the light. I will always love you, Wes.

Here are some shout outs to my core friends and family: Miles Kunisaki, Steven Scott, Kristen Scott, Justin Lee, Troy Boepple, Alexis Sadler, Nick Bradaigh, Chyllis, Chad Scott, Morgan Scott, Nii-Ama Akuete, Tyler Nave, Elena Lacovelli, Matt Baker, the Baker girls, Amanda Freitag, Danielle Kelly, Paul Kelly, Leon Chen, Tara Vega, Amanda Matuk, Jim Clark, Brett Greving, Dale Levitski, CJ Jacobson, Ariane Duarte, Michael Duarte, Kimberly Locke, Janet Annino, David Duncan, Mrs. Arkfeld, Jackie Olensky, Barbie Pritchard, Alan Carter, the Offenbach family, the Padillas, my Kings Hawaiian family, my bread culinary brother—Mark Luker, my media sister—Tinu Rudrakshi Smith, Andrew Stern, Steve Kann, Scott Rodrick, Joy Bauer, Matthew Lyons, Tammy Filler, Michael Lomonaco, Leslie Sbrocco, Phill Wills, Chops, JG, James Agiesta, Ron Krantz, Sister Roma, Telmo Faria, Tony Gemignani, Todd English, John Gidding, Taniya Nayak, Michael Ploetz, Hector Maldonado, Sam Saboura, June Ovens and team, Liam Mayclem, Dan Gordon, Stephen Kellogg, Jon Taffer, Nicole Taffer, Terrance Frazier, Esmeralda Soria, Anthony Contrino, Katie Ryan, Katie Stilo, Mia Mastroianni, and the Tri-Star team. I'd also like to dedicate this book to my dear friend Floyd Cardoz, whom we lost during the Coronavirus pandemic in 2020. You are missed every day.

INDEX